The Secret Societies handbook

LEFT: *Knights Templar*

$\mathfrak{The}$ $\mathfrak{Secret}$ $\mathfrak{Societies}$ $\mathfrak{Handbook}$

CASSELL
ILLUSTRATED

First Published in Great Britain in 2005 by Cassell Illustrated,
A division of Octopus Publishing Group Limited,
2-4 Heron Quays, London E14 4JP

Publisher's Note: The views expressed herein are the personal views of the authors and are not intended to reflect the views of the Publisher.

© 2005 Gusto Company AS

WRITTEN BY Michael Bradley
PHOTOGRAPHY AND ILLUSTRATIONS © Corbis Images/Scanpix,
except pages 13 & 15 © Getty Images/Bridgeman Art Library
EDITED BY Katherine Robinson
PROJECT EDITOR GUSTO COMPANY James Tavendale and Ernesto Gremese
EXECUTIVE EDITORS GUSTO COMPANY James Tavendale and Ernesto Gremese
DESIGNED BY Saroyan Humphrey

A CIP catalogue record for this book is available from the British Library

ISBN 1-84403-416-X
EAN 9781844034161

Printed in China

Introduction

I approached my research for *The Secret Societies Handbook* with the same intellectual smugness with which I read stories about alien abductions or sightings of Elvis Presley. I had given little thought to medieval cabals and ancient secrets, much less a new world order, global economic corruption, covert eugenics programmes, or racist plots to control the world population. Sure, I figured that some politicians were fakes and that life isn't fair, but that was about as far as I had ever gone down the sorry path of blaming all the problems in the world on "them."

Furthermore, I was expecting to dumb down my content to make it fit a simple, sensationalist, tabloid view. It soon became apparent that I had discovered a much more serious and complex story. I used to consider myself to be a fairly perceptive and well-educated citizen, responsible for making my own way in the world and trying not to mess up anyone else's life in the process; after all, we're all just muddling through together, right?

How wrong I was. I now believe that Western history needs to be completely rewritten to tell the hidden story behind our true economic and political global hierarchy. The more I have researched, the more alarming my discoveries have been. I came in contact with an underworld of modern-day "heretics" who dare to believe a different version of reality from the one that has been sold to us for the last 2,000 years. Like most free thinkers, they are quickly discredited by those who wish to maintain the status quo, but slowly, even I have woken up to the possibility that we are not free, that we do not control our own destinies, and that we are the puppets, not the masters.

This handbook will serve you as a reference source for 21 of the world's most dangerous secret societies. At first sight, some of them don't even appear to be "secret." They have websites and noble mission statements, but these are the most impregnable of all. Covert agendas have always been deeply embedded in the "inner circle" of openly respectable societies (in recognition of this, extreme right-wing white-supremacist groups are currently falling over themselves to appear more approachable and peaceful to disguise the fact that their racist agenda is undiminished).

The anti-fascist political commentator Dorothy Thompson once said, "Fear grows in darkness; if you think there's a bogeyman around, turn on the light." I hope this book will briefly illuminate this hidden world and, like a match struck in the dark, give you a brief glimpse of the horrors that really are in front of our faces. The bogeymen are there, all right, lurking somewhere between the myth and the mundane.

Michael Bradley
Hotel da Verrazzano, Via di Bellariva, Florence, 2004

The Assassins

URING THE MIDDLE of the twelfth century, a secretive hashish-smoking Shi'ite Muslim sect in Syria staked its claim to the Islamic Empire with such calculated and ruthless violence that its name is now synonymous with expedient murder. It established a system of underground cells and created a branching pyramid system of agents and spies throughout the Muslim world with a command structure that would be copied by all subsequent secret societies, including the Freemasons and the Templars. They were called the Assassins.

At first they were called the Nizariyah in their attempt to restore Prince Nizar al-Tayyib to the Caliphship of Egypt, whom they proclaimed as the miraculous reincarnation of Isma'il. When this failed they set up a new cycle of Nizariyah imams, which they decided (conveniently) would distinguish themselves from previous imams by actually breaking the established laws of the *shari'ah* (the sacred law, as opposed to Islamic jurisprudence, prescribed by Allah) in preparation for the arrival of *al-Mahdi* (the apocalyptic "chosen one").

This meant the Nizariyah imams could grant themselves license to drink wine and smoke large quantities of hashish and even to kill other Muslims in the pursuit of *jihad* (the holy struggle of Muslims). It wasn't long before they were denounced by orthodox authorities as apostates (non-Muslims) and became marked men.

The Nizariyah moved from Egypt into Syria, where they became known as the "hashshasin" (Assassins)—the Arabic plural for hashish smokers, although some commentators have suggested that "guardians [of the secrets]" is the true origin of the word. Under the leadership of Hasan bin Sabah they conducted a vicious guerrilla war and mounted attacks on Baghdad from their fortress headquarters in the Alamut valley in northern Persia to try to overthrow the Sunni rulers.

In *The History of the Assassins*, Amin Maalouf describes Hasan as "a man of immense culture, a devotee of poetry profoundly interested in the latest advances of science." He drew heavily on the organization and techniques of the *Dar ul Hikmat*

The Assassins' stronghold Alamut

(House of Knowledge), or Grand Lodge of Cairo, when he developed his methods. For more than two centuries the Assassins perfected techniques of murder, weaponry, poisoning, and covert operations that made them the scourge of the Eastern world. Their Alamut fortress has entered into Persian legend as a sumptuous earthly paradise which Marco Polo described after passing that way in 1271:

"In a beautiful valley, enclosed between two lofty mountains, he [Hasan] had formed a luxurious garden stored with every delicious fruit and every fragrant shrub that could be procured. Palaces of various sizes and forms were erected in different parts of the grounds, ornamented with works of gold, with paintings and with furniture of rich silks. By means of small conduits contained in these buildings, streams of wine, milk, honey and some of pure water were seen to flow in every direction. The inhabitants of these places were elegant and beautiful damsels, accomplished in the arts of singing, playing upon all sorts of musical instruments, dancing, and especially those of dalliance and amorous allurement. In order that none without his licence should find their way into this delicious valley, he caused a strong and inexpungible castle to be erected at the opening to it, through which the entry was by a secret passage."

Hasan was said to recruit local youths by drugging them and then transporting them to the valley where, after receiving a glimpse of paradise, they would be thrust back to reality, which would now appear so mundane by comparison that they would willingly join his cause and be prepared to die for the chance of returning to the garden of arcane delights. Once Hasan had recruited his new apprentices, they would then be brainwashed with tricks and drugs into mindless acceptance of his unique personality cult whose motto was "Nothing is forbidden, everything is permitted."

One such illusion, described in Abdel-Rahman's ancient *Art of Imposture,* involved burying a disciple up to his neck, which would then be daubed with blood; this apparently dismembered head would then describe the delights of paradise to the initiates.

Afterward the unfortunate disciple would secretly be beheaded and placed on public view to complete the trickery.

According to Arkon Daraul in *A History of Secret Societies*, there were three degrees of followers: "Missionaries (Dayes), Friends (Rafiq) who were disciples, and Fidavis, devotees. The last group . . . were the trained killers. Fidavis wore white, with a girdle, cap or boots of red. In addition to careful coaching in where and when to place the dagger in the victim's bosom, they were trained in such things as languages, the dress and manners of monks, merchants and soldiers, any of whom they were ready to impersonate in carrying out their missions."

An Assassin would be instructed to perform a killing with the words: "Where do you come from?" He would reply "From Paradise," then receive his instructions: "Go then and slay a man I shall name. When you return you shall again dwell in Paradise. Fear not death because the Angels of Allah will transport you nevertheless to Paradise."

The Assassins' influence spread throughout Persia and Iraq until the middle of the thirteenth century when the sect gradually imploded after Hasan was murdered by his son, Mohammed, who was in turn dispatched by his own son. The Alamut fortress was captured by the Mongols in 1256, marking the beginning of the end of the Assassins as a cohesive military force until the early sixteenth century when the Ottomans destroyed their last strongholds in Syria. However, the dynasty of Nizari Isma'ilite Imams has continued in modern branches of Islam through the Aga Khan, although modern Isma'ilites have dropped the title "Assassins" and most accept the Qur'an's message of tolerance.

The Bilderbergers

The Bilderberg Hotel in Holland

T HE BILDERBERGER GROUP is named after the hotel in Oosterbeek, Holland, where it met in the early years of its existence after its creation in 1954. Officially it has no name, but then "officially" it doesn't exist. In reality it is composed of more than 100 of the global power elite— international financiers, multinational bosses, and political leaders and European royalty, allededly including Prince Charles, Queen Sophia of Spain, and Queen Beatrix of the Netherlands. It is said that the two leading power brokers are the American Rockefeller family and the European Rothschilds.

Each year they meet for four days at a secret location in Europe or the United States. The 2003 gathering took place between May 15 and 18 at the luxurious and historic Trianon Palace at Versailles, but it was barely mentioned in the press. This is because top media figures are either members or on the guest list. The publisher of the *Washington Post* attends every

Margaret Thatcher and Lord Carrington

meeting and the news chiefs of the *New York Times,* the *Los Angeles Times,* and TV networks have also taken part on the understanding that discussions are off the record. As French broadcaster Thierry de Segonzac put it, "the Bilderbergers are too powerful and omnipresent to be exposed."

The meetings were chaired by former Nazi SS officer Prince Bernhard of the Netherlands until his resignation in 1976 following his involvement in the Lockheed Scandal. The current chair is Lord Peter Carrington, a former British government cabinet minister and secretary general of NATO, who is connected to the Rothschild family through marriage.

Reporter Emma Jane Kirby has described the Bilderberger Group as "an extremely influential lobbying group with a good deal of political clout on both sides of the Atlantic." This may be hugely understating their influence. A unified Europe, the Treaty of Rome, the single European currency, the ending of the Cold

War, the North American Free Trade Agreement (NAFTA), the Brady plan (President Reagan's pledge to provide $50 billion to Third World and Communist countries), and the ousting of Margaret Thatcher as prime minister of Britain because she resisted the European super state are just a few of the ideas that materialized at Bilderberger meetings.

Like its related groups the Trilateral Commission (see page 136) and the Council on Foreign Relations (see page 36), the Bilderberger aim is a one-world government and to promote the idea that national sovereignty is antiquated and regressive. Author Neal Wilgus has described them as a "sort of unofficial CFR, expanded to an international scale." Many critics believe they have the clout to mastermind world events and engineer policies and international projects that increase their wealth and power. If power is what they seek, then one group of politicians would be easier to bribe, corrupt, and influence than those of several countries. These high priests of globalization benefit greatly from "internationalism" since it inevitably leads to large-scale, publicly funded projects that can be used to increase the Bilderbergers' wealth and power (for example sending billions in financial aid to the former Soviet Union and then extracting natural resources at rock-bottom prices; disastrous International Monetary Fund policies that deliberately keep Third World Countries crippled and powerless).

Each year, in addition to the core membership, a few ambitious new faces are invited, selected when they seem in a promising political position, dropped when they cease to be of use. Douglas Wilder, the first black United States governor was invited when his political career looked set to go stratospheric, but in 1984 when he failed to gain more than one percent of the vote in the Democratic presidential primary, he was removed from the guest list. However, the Bilderbergers struck lucky in 1991 when they invited the governor of Arkansas, Bill Clinton, into their fold at their confab in Baden Baden, Germany. A year later he was elected president.

It is alleged that the Bilderbergers have had every president since the early 1970s in their pocket. Gerald Ford was a Bilderberger; Jimmy Carter and his vice president Walter Mondale were members of the Trilateral Commission. During the 1980 primaries Ronald Reagan said he would have nothing to do with the Trilaterals, but later appointed Trilateralist George Bush his vice president. His son George W. Bush is not connected to these groups, but several in his administration are Bilderberger attendees.

Former British intelligence officer Dr. John Coleman claims that the conference is sanctioned by Britain's MI6 with authority from the Royal Institute of International Affairs (of which Lord Carrington is the president). In America, the CIA provides intelligence and security for the meetings. This isn't surprising since the framework for the CIA—the Office of Strategic Services (OSS) was built by none other than John J. McCloy, a former Chairman of the Council on Foreign Relations, and Chairman of the Rockefeller Chase Manhattan Bank.

The fact that the police arrest and charge card-carrying journalists who attempt to expose them is clear evidence that Bilderberger meetings are more than a "private" event. The organization and security cordon surrounding them makes White House security look like the Home Guard. In Versaille the security perimeter was unprecedented and local residents had their movements restricted by Bilderberger security and the French military, although no one was given a satisfactory explanation, and nothing appeared in the press.

A member of the European Commission and Bilderberger attendee, Mario Monti, recently played down the conferences saying, "The participants attend meetings in a private capacity and the statements which they make are not binding on the [European] Commission; no resolutions are passed, no votes are taken and no political communiques are issued." The reality is that the Bilderbergers' off-the-record briefings are way above democracy and the law.

The Bohemian Club

ORMED IN 1872 by five San Francisco journalists as a male-only drinking club, today it is one of the most prestigious (and as some claim, dissolute) societies in the United States. Its waiting list is in the hundreds, and its membership includes top Republicans and many directors, global financiers, and the chief executive officers of many Fortune 1000 companies.

Members past and present include every Republican president since Herbert Hoover (including Richard Nixon, Ronald Reagan, and George W. Bush), William F. Buckley Jr., Frank Borman, Justin Dart, William Randolph Hearst Jr., Caspar Weinberger, Charles Percy, George Schultz, Edward Teller, Merv Griffin, Colin Powell, Henry Kissinger, and Newt Gingrich.

Mary Moore, a spokesperson for the Bohemian Group Action Network, has described it as "one of the most elite organizations on the planet."

Every fall the Bohemian Club's Annual Summer Encampment (which Herbert Hoover described as "the greatest men's party on earth") is held at the 2,700-acre Bohemian Grove in Monte Rio, about 70 miles north of San Francisco. They meet to uphold what they call "the spirit of Bohemia": an opportunity for the most powerful men in the United States and a handful of other countries to gather around the campfire and network in the best tradition of (largely) white male elitism. It is the smoked-filled room transported outdoors into the woods.

Many key political decisions are made not in Congress, but here, off-the-record, in private. Its Shakespearean motto, "weaving spiders come not here," would appear to discourage members from intrigue and back-room deals, but the reality is quite the opposite. For example, it was at the Grove in 1967 that Ronald Reagan agreed with Richard Nixon to stay out of the forthcoming presidential nominations.

One of the features of the retreat is the daily lakeside talks where important speakers address geopolitical issues away from public scrutiny and the democratic process. Peter Phillips, Associate Professor of Sociology at Sonoma State University, indicates these have included topics such as the "dangers of multi-culturalism, Afro-centrism, and the loss of family boundaries" and expresses sentiments such as the importance of elites to define themselves and set values or "standards of authority" to control the "unqualified" masses.

Within the Grove's grounds are more than 100 separate camps with names such as Whiskey Flat, Toyland, Owl's Nest, Hill Billies, and Cave Man's, each with its own kitchen, bar, and sleeping quarters (tents and redwood cabins). One of the main camp events is the Grove play, written exclusively for the club, or drawn from Shakespeare or Greek mythology, with all the female roles played by men in drag.

The secrecy of the Grove has inevitably encouraged wild speculation about what really goes on there. At the extreme end of the spectrum of criticism against the club are rumours of bizarre rites and reports of immoral practices involving mind control and prostitution. Reporter Alex Jones claims to have infiltrated the Bohemian Grove with a hidden digital video camera and captured arcane rituals on tape (for more information see his website www.infowars.com). He reports having evidence of an occult ritual involving the worship of a giant stone effigy called the Great Owl of Bohemia.

At the very least the Bohemian Club is an opportunity for the world's movers and shakers to forge connections, build insider ties and spread policy information well away from the eyes and ears of the citizens whose interests they claim to represent. The nefarious rumours may be the product of overripe imaginations or another example of secrecy spawning fears of corruption; it may even be a smoke screen to blind us to the possibility that democracy is gradually being eroded.

The Club of Rome

ORMED IN 1968 by Italian industrialist Aurelio Peccei, the Club of Rome can be variously described as a Hamburg-based global think tank or, depending on your point of view, another elite cabal of globalist one-worlders trying to manipulate international politics and economics through their close ties with the ruling elite, the World Bank, and the International Monetary Fund.

On its website (www.clubofrome.org) it sets out its mission "to act as an independent, global, non official catalyst of change" through "the identification of the most crucial problems facing humanity, their analysis in the global context of the world-wide problematique, the research of future alternative solutions and the elaboration of scenarios for the future" and "the communication of such problems to the most important public and private decision-makers as well as to the general public."

All well and good. A "full" list of names and addresses of its hundred or so members (active, associate, and honorary) are printed on the website (except for its host of dominant figures in the world establishment), along with details of its conferences and numerous research papers.

The Club of Rome became well known in 1972 with its publication of *The Limits to Growth* that warned that the Earth's resources were finite and highlighted the negative consequences of a rapidly growing global population. The book became an instant best seller, was translated in 30 languages, and sold more than four million copies.

Unfortunately it was these revelations that have since sparked debate amongst conspiracy theorists that the Club of Rome has been instrumental in one of the biggest genocides the world has ever known: namely, the spread of AIDS, which some sources claim is a man-made virus developed as a result of top secret recommendations made by the Club of Rome to the ruling elite (the CIA and the Bilderberg Group, see page 18).

This alleged plan was to target "undesirable elements of society" for extermination, including black, Hispanic, and

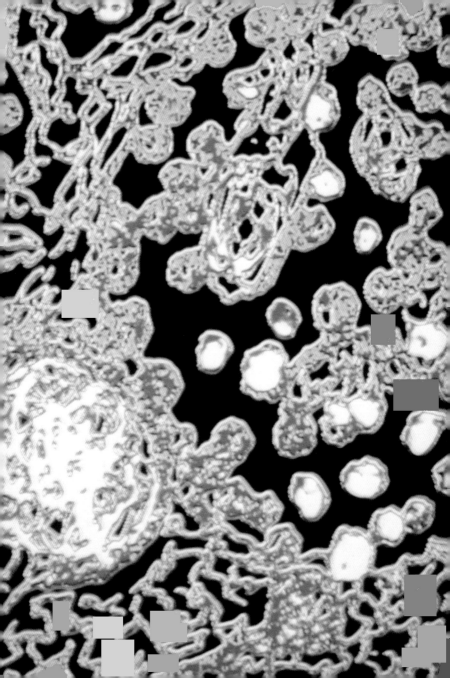

homosexual communities. According to William Cooper (see www.thewatcherfiles.com/cooper/aids.htm) who "was killed on November 5th 2001 by law enforcement . . . The name of the project that developed AIDS is MK-NAOMI. The African continent was infected via smallpox vaccine in 1977. The United States population was infected in 1978 with the hepatitis B vaccine through the Centers for Disease Control and the New York Blood Center."

It wasn't the first time that calls had been made for population control. In 1948 George W. McKennan from the United States State Department issued Foreign Policy Statement-21 (FPS-21) highlighting the necessity for the United States to "devise a scheme" to deal with "burgeoning populations." On March 16, 1970, President Richard Nixon allegedly signed off law PL91-213 that authorizes "stabilization" of the population of Sub-Saharan Africa and appointed John D. Rockefeller III to oversee this "problem."

Neither was MK-NAOMI the first CIA research programme designed to produce and test drugs and biological agents. In 1953 a 10-year project called MK-ULTRA developed nerve agents for mind control and behaviour modification. This was followed by MK-SEARCH and MK-OFTEN. Then, in 1969, Dr. Robert MacMahan of the Department of Defense requested $10 million from Congress to develop, within 5 to 10 years, a synthetic biological agent to which no natural immunity exists. The funding was granted in 1970 under H.R. 15090 and financed the MK-NAOMI project that used sub-molecular biology techniques to produce AIDS-like retroviruses. At this time the CIA was also exploring the viability of "ethnic weapons" that could selectively target specific ethnic groups based on genetic differences and variations in DNA. All these experiments took place at the Special Operations Division at Fort Detrick in Frederick, Maryland. A vital piece of proof cited by those who believe that AIDS is man-made is a 1971 AIDS flowchart (page 61 of Progress Report #8) that is said to coordinate more than 20,000 scientific papers and 15 years of research into a federal programme to develop a virus that shows an identical match to the epidemiology of AIDS.

Well-documented facts have already been made public under the Freedom of Information Act about the sordid history of United States human experimentation over the last 70 years.

In the 1930s American soldiers and civilian hospital patients were unwittingly used as guinea pigs in a series of radiation exposure experiments. Also in the 1930s, the Tuskegee Syphilis Study began tracking 200 black men diagnosed with syphilis who were never informed of their illness so that the long-term effects of the disease could be observed. A Senate committee that investigated the practices of MK-ULTRA has concluded, "From its beginning in the early 1950s until its termination in 1963, the program of surreptitious administration of LSD to unwitting non-volunteer human subjects demonstrates a failure of the CIA's leadership to pay adequate attention to the rights of individuals and to provide effective guidance to CIA employees. Though it was known that the testing was dangerous, the lives of subjects were placed in jeopardy and were ignored. . . . Although it was clear that the laws of the United States were being violated, the testing continued." Even as recently as the last Gulf War, soldiers were given a cocktail of experimental drugs that left thousands suffering from Gulf War Syndrome.

On October 3, 1995, President Clinton finally admitted that the radiation exposure experiments took place and that the United States government was liable for compensation.

Meanwhile AIDS, largely under control in the West, continues to spread across the African continent. It matters not that *The Limits to Growth* has since been debunked as a fraudulent document that, according to one of the club's directors, used a misleading computer model. Of the 50 million people who have died of AIDS during the last 25 years, over 70 percent were from Africa and the epidemic there is growing. The origins of AIDS are still largely shrouded in mystery, but one thing is certain: whatever the truth, the urgent recommendations made by the Club of Rome are being played out today with ruthless and exponential efficiency.

Council ^{on} Foreign Relations

)))HAT BEGAN AS a series of meetings organized by Colonel Edward Mandell House, President Woodrow Wilson's confidential adviser during World War I, is now widely acknowledged to be the biggest globalist secret society—the Council on Foreign Relations (CFR).

In New York in 1917, Wilson assembled about 100 important men to discuss a peace settlement and postwar plans. The self-styled "inquiry" wrote most of Woodrow Wilson's 14 points, which he put before Congress in January 1918. They proposed the removal of "all economic barriers" between nations, free trade, and the formation of a "general association of nations" (the League of Nations). Wilson's peace terms formed the basis of the Treaty of Versailles that required Germany to pay crippling reparations, and caused the depression that fostered Adolf Hitler's rise to power.

Wilson's peace plans were rejected by the United States Senate, which was wary of anything that smacked of a supernational organization. However, Colonel House and the British and American peace conference delegates met again in Paris in May 1919 and agreed to form an Institute of International Affairs with the aim of steering the world towards the acceptance of a one-world government. Its British branch is called the Royal Institute of International Affairs, and the United States branch was constructed on July 21, 1921, as the Council on Foreign Relations. One of CFR's rules states that any member divulging information about CFR meetings will lose membership.

The Harold Pratt House in New York City is the CFR headquarters and has lavishly housed the New York liberal elite since it was donated in 1945 by the Pratt family of Rockefeller's Standard Oil. Originally there were about 1,600 members, but this has grown to 3,300 as influential figures in finance, politics, communications, and academia have swelled its ranks after careful selection and rigorous screening.

Original CFR members included Elihu Root, John Foster Dulles, and Christian Herter, all three of whom served as secretary of state; also Dulles' brother Allen Dulles, who later became the director of the CIA, was a member. Since then nearly every one of Dulles' successors has been a CFR member, including George Bush and William Casey. Founder members John W. Davis and Russell Leffingwell were financier J.P. Morgan's right-hand men, and many of the other early members had strong links with him, so CFR policy must have served Morgan's interests and allegedly still does.

Not only does the CFR run the CIA, they also control the State Department. This started when President Truman established the Psychological Strategy Board (PSB) to coordinate psycho-political operations. It was headed by CFR members Gordon Gray and Henry Kissinger. The PSB has close links with the State Department and CIA. Eisenhower changed its name to the Operations Coordination Board (OCB), and when President Kennedy abolished it, the OCB became an ad hoc committee called the Special Group which continues today. It is run by CFR members.

In February 1941 the CFR took control of the State Department with the establishment of the Division of Special Research, forming groups of experts to mastermind research into security, armaments, economics, and politics. Like the PSB and OCB, the Division of Special Research is run by CFR cronies.

Originally CFR funding came from bankers and financiers, including Morgan, Rockefeller, and Otto Kahn, and today comes from the State Department and corporations, including Xerox, General Motors,

Texaco, and the Rockefeller Brothers Fund. Like the Bilderbergers, albeit with less secrecy, the CFR communicates its ideas through conferences and smaller luncheon or dinner meetings. It also acts as a think tank to produce research to further its globalist agenda. The CFR's publication *Foreign Affairs* is the public mouthpiece. It is widely acknowledged that just as Broadway shows rise or fall on the opinion of the *New York Times* critic, ideas rarely make it into United States government foreign policy until they have gained approval in this CFR club magazine.

Admiral Chester Ward, a retired senior figure in the United States Navy and CFR member, co-authored a book in 1975 with Phyllis Schafly called *Kissinger on the Couch* in which he states, "Once the ruling members of the CFR have decided that the United States government should adopt a particular policy, the very substantial research facilities of the CFR are put to work to develop arguments, intellectual and emotional, to support the new policy, and to confound and discredit, intellectually and politically, any opposition."

Henry Kissinger rose to prominence by exploiting his CFR connections, which included David Rockefeller. Through the CFR he gained inside knowledge of the Atomic Energy Commission, the military, the CIA, and the State Department to write his best-selling book *Nuclear Weapons and Foreign Policy*, which put forth the case that a nuclear war might be "winnable."

The CFR has placed 100 of its members in every presidential administration since Woodrow Wilson. Both the Republican George W. Bush and his Democrat opponent in the 2000 election, Al Gore, are CFR men, and the Clinton administration included more than 100 CFR members, many of whom have become foreign ambassadors to spread the good news about federalism and globalism.

Some critics of the CFR claim that the Marshall Plan and the subsequent North Atlantic Treaty Organization (NATO) came into being after an "anonymous" letter that appeared in *Foreign Affairs* gave Truman the nod to take a hard line against

President Richard Nixon and Henry Kissinger

the threat of Soviet expansion. Ever since, despite the collapse of Soviet Communism, the attitude towards armaments has been spend, spend, spend.

Evidently the prudent words of Thomas Jefferson have been long forgotten: "I place economy among the first and most important of republican virtues, and public debt as the greatest of dangers to be feared."

Essex Junto

*T*HE ESSEX JUNTO were a group of Federalists from New England who opposed Thomas Jefferson's election in 1800 and 1804. They included Massachusetts Senator George Cabot, Judge John Lowell, former Secretary of State Timothy Pickering, Stephen Higginson, Massachusetts Supreme Court Justice Theophilus Parsons, and Judge Tapping Reeve, as well as the Forbes, Cushing, Perkins, Sturgis, and Paine families.

Jefferson was widely popular after the Louisiana Purchase and the repeal of excise tax on whisky. The Essex Junto began plotting before the elections to remove their states from the Union. They wanted to create a Northern Confederacy from the states of Massachusetts, Rhode Island, Connecticut, New Hampshire, Vermont, New York, and New Jersey.

They planned to do this by putting up their own candidate for the governorship of New York (Aaron Burr) who, once elected, would lead the state out of the Union. Burr was unsuccessful, largely due to the manoeuvrings of United States nationalist leader and former Treasury Secretary Alexander Hamilton, who gave his support to Jefferson. Hamilton called Burr "a dangerous man, and one who ought not to be trusted with the reins of government." Hamilton was murdered in July 1804 in a duel set up by Burr, who then continued in his abortive secret plan to form a new republic in the southwest composed of southern United States territory and Spanish Mexico.

The Essex Junto wanted to secede from the United States because Jefferson's policies damaged their own illegal business interests. The Cabot, Lowell, and Higginson families were smuggler millionaires whose fortune came from the Turkish opium trade to China. They had been forced out of the slave trade by United States law and the Caribbean slave revolts, and didn't want to see their other interests destroyed. Financed by Britain's Baring's Bank, Connecticut was the heart of the United States opium racket by the 1830s. The Cabots, Lowells, and other blue-blood families also controlled and patronized Harvard.

In *Treason in America*, Anton Chaitkin claims the Essex Junto was "working in close collaboration with agents of the British

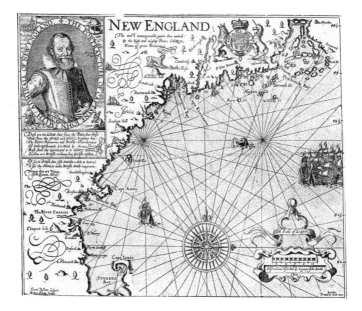

Map of New England

Secret Service (SIS)" and most importantly with "British SIS intelligence operative Sir John Robison . . . from then to the present day, the family traditions and financial connections of those circles have been intimately associated with the British [SIS]." This is the same John Robison who, in 1789, wrote *Proofs of a Conspiracy* in which he exposes the Illuminati (see page 62), about whom he wrote:

"Their first and immediate aim is to get the possession of riches, power, and influence, without industry; and, to accomplish this, they want to abolish Christianity; and then dissolute manners and universal profligacy will procure them the adherents of all the wicked, and enable them to overturn all the civil governments of Europe; after which they will think of farther conquests, and extend their operations to the other quarters of the globe, till they have reduced mankind to the state of one indistinguishable chaotic mass."

Chaitkin believes this book to be "the source of the Illuminati myth." He makes the case for this being a "red herring intended to deflect attention away from the treasonous horde which he orchestrated." This idea is reinforced in Robert Alan Goldberg's book *Enemies Within*:

"Writing in the aftermath of the French Revolution, these monarchists had created a counterhistory in defense of the aristocracy . . . The Revolution, they argued, was not rooted in poverty and despotism. Rather than a rising of the masses, it was the work of Adam Weishaupt's Illuminati, a secret society that plotted to destroy all civil and religious authority and abolish marriage, the family, and private property."

It makes absolute sense that the British Secret Service should be closely linked to any plot that threatened the American Union and could reverse the effects of the American Revolution.

As Jeffrey Brackeen points out in *The Seventh Trumpet*, "Industrialization, beginning in the late 1700s, created a demand for new markets and increased raw materials; both demands spurred accelerated expansion of empire. Wealthy investors amassed fortunes by setting up large-scale industrial and trading operations, leading to the emergence of an influential capitalist elite. Like any other elite, capitalists used their wealth and influence to further their own interests however they could."

The fact that the Essex Junto were unsuccessful does not lessen the important fact that 200 years ago a powerful elite conspired to change the course of a nation's history in order to further its own business interests. It is somehow easier to believe in the existence of such a secret cabal when it has long passed into history, but it is much harder to admit to ourselves (or prove) that the same thing is happening today. Only this time it is on a global scale.

Freemasonry

George Washington as a Freemason

$\mathfrak{I}$F THERE REALLY is a covert plot to take over the world, many suspect that the Masons thought of it first.

Freemasonry is the world's oldest and largest fraternity. In any close study of secret societies they appear over and over again, intertwined with most of the other secret occult orders, and most likely predating them all.

Today, despite the Masons' many acts of public service, conspiracy theorists seem drawn towards them. In fact, the Freemasons have found their bad press so difficult to shake that they have recently recruited a public relations agency to improve their image and the public perception of, at best, rampant behind-the-scenes back scratching and, at worst, a demonic will to power.

Centuries ago the masons were skilled stone-workers and architects. Their know-how and craftsmanship were at the cutting edge of technology, so it is understandable that they should have formed into secretive guilds to protect and hand down their esoteric knowledge. They employed techniques that dated back to those used by the guilds of masons in ancient Egypt and Greece.

It was a Masonic guild in northern Italy that first adopted the name "Freemasons" in the Middle Ages, but like the Knights Templar (see page 68), they claim lineage to the warrior knights of the Crusades and Godfrey de Bouillon, the leader of the First Crusade (see page 110, Priory of Sion), and beyond to the construction of the Tower of Babel and King Solomon's Temple in Jerusalem.

The most likely explanation is that Freemasonry grew from several different sources that merged and developed over time. It could also be argued however that the modern order dates to 1717 when four lodges in Great Britain formed the first United Grand Lodge. The order was spread worldwide by the British Empire, especially through Cecil Rhodes's Round Table (see page 124).

However, Knight and Lomas in *The Hiram Key* place the origin at the construction of the Rosslyn Chapel near Edinburgh, Scotland, in the mid-fifteenth century. Many of the Masonic

A Freemason initiation ceremony

records were destroyed or disbursed during the reformation, and this, combined with deliberate misinformation from the Masons and speculation from outsiders, has made it almost impossible to find the truth. Knight and Lomas go so far as to suggest that even the Masons themselves no longer have access to their own "true secrets," and some have nicknamed them the "Mafia of the Mediocre," suggesting that nepotism is now their only sovereignty.

The extent of their power today is still a mystery, but you don't have to look far to see evidence of their past influence. Every strata of Masonry is dense with symbolism and allegory. More than half of the Founding Fathers were Masons, and a

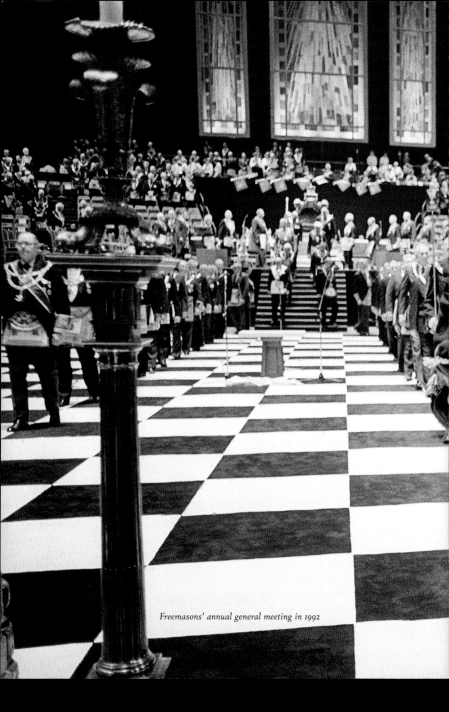

Freemasons' annual general meeting in 1992

RIGHT: *Bunch of Grapes tavern,*
alleged birthplace of Freemasonry in
the United States.

close examination of a map of Washington, D.C., reveals that they hid their two most important occult symbols, the pentagram (five-pointed star) and the "Square and Compass," at the heart of the United States.

Beginning at the White House, draw a straight line to Scott Circle. From there continue to Washington Circle and on to Mount Vernon Square, Dupont Circle, and back to the White House. You will be confronted with the most potent pentagram in the occult symbolic repertoire—the demonic "Goathead." Four upper points representing the elements of Fire, Water, Earth, and Air, and the bottom point (The White House) the mind of Lucifer. This same site forms the upper tip of a compass, the arm extending down Pennsylvania Avenue to the Capitol (the top of the compass) and then out again down Maryland Avenue in a second arm that ends at the Jefferson Memorial.

The Washington Monument, which lies directly west of the Capitol, has been identified as the most significant occult symbol of all—an obelisk set inside a circle—embodying the spirit of the ancient Egyptian sun god Ra and commemorating the first United States president, who was a high-ranking Mason.

Evidence of Masonic symbols and influence surround us, even on the back of the United States dollar bill: the all-seeing eye, the pyramid, the stars above the eagle's head in the shape of a pentagram, and the mottos *e pluribus unum* (out of many, one) and *novus ordo seclorum* (a new order of the ages).

Today there are more than six million Freemasons with 100,000 lodges worldwide. Though, much like the Round Table and the Optimists, the rank and file see it as little more than an opportunity for social networking, although they must swear "ever to conceal, never to reveal."

But, as Manly Palmer Hall, an honorary thirty-third degree Mason, reveals in *The Lost Keys Of Freemasonry*, "Freemasonry is a fraternity within a fraternity—an outer organization concealing

THE SITE OF THE
BUNCH OF GRAPES TAVERN
HERE ON 30TH OF JULY 1733
WAS INSTITUTED UNDER CHARTER FROM
THE GRAND LODGE OF ENGLAND
THE FIRST REGULARLY CONSTITUTED LODGE
OF FREE AND ACCEPTED MASONS IN AMERICA
NOW ST JOHN'S LODGE OF BOSTON

HERE IN 1786 WAS ORGANIZED THE OHIO COMPANY
PIONEER IN THE DEVELOPMENT OF THE GREAT WEST
UNDER THE LEADERSHIP OF GENERAL RUFUS PUTNAM
FIRST TOWNSHIP LAID OUT AT MARIETTA OHIO

THIS TABLET PLACED BY THE CITY OF BOSTON
30TH OF JULY 1925

an inner brotherhood of the elect . . . the one visible and the other invisible. The visible society is a splendid camaraderie of 'free and accepted men' . . . the invisible society is a secret and most august fraternity whose members are dedicated to the service of an . . . *arcanum arcandrum* [a sacred secret]."

Those who maintain that this "inner brotherhood" operates outside the law have touched on several scandals during the past 40 years. In the 1970s much of the corruption uncovered in the Flying Squad at Britain's Scotland Yard was attributed to Masonic allegiances. Then on June 18, 1982, Italian financier Roberto Calvi was found hanging from Blackfriars Bridge in London. He was nicknamed "God's banker" because of his links with the Vatican and the Italian Mafia. The case has recently been reopened to explore the involvement in his murder of the now defunct P2 "Propaganda Due" Masonic lodge in Italy, and whether Calvi died for mishandling Mafia money and blackmailing P2 members.

Joseph Fort Newton, an Episcopal minister and authority on the Masons, described Masonry as "religion—not a church but a worship in which men of all religions may unite." The Freemasonry draws its metaphysical beliefs not from the Bible (referred to as "The Great Light"), but from the Kabbala, a medieval Hebrew book of mysticism and magic. (Belief in a Supreme Being or "Great Architect of the Universe" is the prime requirement for membership. It doesn't matter who your Supreme Being is—presumably even Satan would qualify.)

Their public motto is "morality in which all men agree, that is, to be good men and true." There are three basic lodges: the lowest is the Blue Lodge for initiates, divided into three degrees—Entered Apprentice, Fellow Craft, and Master Mason; the next is the York Rite split into 10 degrees; finally the Scottish Rite has a total of 32 degrees of initiation, and whoever is invited into the thirty-third degree reaches the symbolic head atop the 32 vertebrae in the human spine. Many Masonic commentators claim Britain's Grand Master (thirty-third degree) Mason is Prince Michael of Kent. Anyone reaching the thirty-second degree may join the Shriners (Ancient Arabic Order of the Nobles of the Mystic Shrine). Beyond that, the hierarchy disappears from public view into an unknown number of secret levels.

Entry into each degree is accompanied by an initiation ritual and an oath. Clearly, despite its recent attempts to appear more transparent, Masonry is still as opaque and mercurial as it has always been, as shown by this fragment of the Entered Apprentice oath:

"I most solemnly and sincerely promise and swear, that I will always hail, ever conceal, and never reveal, any of the arts, parts or points of the hidden mysteries of ancient Freemasonry . . . under no less a penalty than that of having my throat cut across, my tongue torn out by its roots, and buried in the rough sand of the sea at low water mark where the tide ebbs and flows twice in twenty-four hours, should I ever knowingly or willingly violate my solemn oath and obligation as an Entered Apprentice Mason. So help me, God."

The Golden Dawn

*T*HE HERMETIC ORDER of the Golden Dawn was founded in 1888 in Great Britain by three Freemasons: William Wynn Westcott, William Robert Woodman, and Samuel Liddell MacGregor Mathers. Although small (it attracted just more than 300 initiates), it included such luminaries as Aleister Crowley, Aubrey Beardsley, and William Butler Yeats and shone briefly as the most significant order to emerge from the nineteenth-century occult revival, possessing one of the greatest ever collections of Western magical knowledge, before bitter leadership rivalry led to its closure in 1914.

Initially it drew upon five Masonic rituals recorded in coded fragments in manuscripts that had come into the possession of London Coroner William Wynn Westcott, along with a letter instructing anyone requiring further information to contact Sapiens Dominabitur Astris ("the wise one will be ruled by the stars") through Fraulein Anna Sprengel, the Imperatrix of the L. L. L. (Licht, Liebe, und Leben, or Light, Love, and Life) branch of German Rosicrucianism. It was on the basis of this dubious pedigree—most likely drawn from Westcott's fertile imagination, although he claimed to have received it from a fellow Mason who had found it in a London book shop—that Die Goldene Dammerung (the Golden Dawn) drew its authority and gained "permission" to convene the Isis-Urania Temple at 17 Fitzroy Street, London.

Samuel Liddell MacGregor Mathers emerged as the most charismatic and eccentric character of the threesome (he had inserted the "MacGregor" into his name because of his deep romantic connection to the Scottish clans). He quickly became the driving force behind the order's structure through his tireless research to expand the ritual fragments into a cohesive metaphysical system. A devoted scholar of old magical texts, he succeeded in combining a complex body of teaching into a workable whole, drawing on the magic of French occultist Alphonse Louis Constant (Magus Eliphas Levi); Kabbalistic cosmology; the Tarot; the impenetrable alchemical and necromantic rites of the medieval grimoires and Eastern mysticism; and Babylonian, Greek, Egyptian, Hindu, and Buddhist mythology.

The inevitable hierarchical structure of the Golden Dawn consisted of 10 degrees of magical attainment, starting with the Neophyte and progressing to the Ipsissimus. They were based on the 10 degrees of the Sephiroth or spheres—interrelated divine emanations from the Kabbala. Members sought "to prosecute the Great Work: which is to obtain control of the nature and power of [one's] own being," and progressed up the degrees by studying and performing Masonic rituals in specially designed temples named after the Egyptian deities. The degrees were divided into three orders: the Outer (Golden Dawn), Second (Red Rose and Golden Cross), and Third (Silver Star). The founders were Chiefs of the Second Order, while the Third Order was occupied solely by entities inhabiting the astral plane who directed their activities.

Unfortunately, the organization was characterized by rampant in-fighting among its prominent members. Woodman died in 1891 and wasn't replaced, leaving the two enormous egos of Mathers and Westcott to battle it out. Mathers moved to Paris to set up his own lodge, and the whole enterprise only survived at all because of the patronage of one of its wealthy members, Annie Horniman, though she withdrew funding in 1896 after being expelled from the Order for disputing Mathers' claim that the Secret Chiefs on the astral plane had invited him into the Third Order. He also claimed that his wife Mina received counsel from the Third Order via clairaudience and supernormal hearing. The following year Westcott resigned over allegations that he had faked the founding manuscripts.

Mathers then devoted himself to translating the Hebrew grimoire *The Book of the Sacred Magic of Abra-Melin the Mage*, which he published in 1898, claiming it was inhabited by a metaphysical entity.

That year, recent Cambridge University graduate Aleister Crowley, who was already an expert in occult science, having rejected the determinism of his strict Plymouth Brethren upbringing, joined the society and sided with the Mathers camp. However, he alienated most of the other members with his outrageous and criminal behavior, sexual indiscretions, and almost superhuman will to power. He took the motto Perdurabo ("I will endure to the end") and was therefore known as Frater Perdurabo.

Within six months Mathers had fast-tracked his new ally to the level of Adeptus Minor of the Second Order, but the London Lodge, then under the leadership of Florence Farr, refused to recognize his advancement. Eventually even Crowley and Mathers fell out with each other and were expelled from the order after trying to harm each other in a magic showdown allegedly involving astral vampires and armies of demons led by Beelzebub. W. B. Yeats took control of the Second Order, and Crowley sought revenge by publishing the Golden Dawn's secrets in 10 editions of his magazine, *The Equinox*.

In the early years of the twentieth century, the Golden Dawn broke apart into several splinter groups which lingered on into the 1930s, including Alpha et Omega (Mathers), Stella Matutina ("Morning Star"—Yeats), Astrum Argenteum (Crowley), Holy Order of the Golden Dawn, and Fraternity of the Inner Light. In 1937 a Stella Matutina member, Israel Regardie, published a massive four-volume account of the rituals, which generated another flowering of subsects and magical misanthropes, so that incarnations of the Golden Dawn still exist today.

The Golden Dawn Research Centre (www.golden-dawn.org) "is a resource for serious students who desire a deeper understanding of the Classical Golden Dawn's teachings and practices." It rightly describes the order as "the most influential force in the modern rebirth of the Western Esoteric Tradition" and on its FAQ page addresses the issue of secrecy:

"Secrecy is necessary in that individual rights and privacy must at all times be maintained, especially since members may work in sensitive environments where public knowledge of their membership could cause problems. There is, however, another important reason for secrecy. It revolves around a Hermetic principle in which the alchemical process requires a closed container, to be 'Hermetically Sealed.'"

The Illuminati

*T*HE MOST POWERFUL secret society of them all, it controls the destiny of the world and seeks to form first a federal Europe, then a single world government. Today it is allegedly the personal coven of the Rothschilds—the richest family on the planet.

Its founder, Dr. Adam Weishaupt, was born on February 6, 1748, the son of a Jewish rabbi. After his father died he converted to Catholicism and was trained by the Jesuits. He later became an atheist and always retained a deep hatred of the Jesuits. Weishaupt founded the Illuminati in order to fight the oppression of religion, destroy the Church, and create a one-world government. He wanted to replace Christianity with a "religion" of reason to end war, ignorance, and the struggle for power. But first he recognized his need to gain huge power in order to put his plan into action. Unfortunately for the world, he has succeeded.

The Illuminati was to be a secret coalition of liberalism and the furthering of knowledge. Weishaupt studied anti-Christian doctrines, astrology, medicine, and the occult. He was also influenced by the secret cult of the Pythagoreans who believed that men and women should pool their belongings (later to become the basic philosophy of Communism). He also studied the Masons (and was later to form an alliance with them). On May 1, 1776, under the direction of the newly formed House of Rothschild, he formed the secret Order of the Illuminati ("enlightened ones"), the name said to be derived from Luciferian teachings (Lucifer means "Bearer of Light"). He started with just five members. The organization copied the hierarchical structure of the Jesuits and the Freemasons and ever since, the Illuminati has used a variety of tactics to motivate, blackmail, and manipulate people in the name of enlightenment, freedom, and emancipation in order to maintain power.

All members are given a classical name. The early members were called Spartacus, Cato, Lucian, Pythagoras, Marius, Diomedes, Ajar, Mohomed, and Sylla, and their headquarters were in Munich. In 1777 they joined and soon took control of the Masonic lodge there. Within four years there were 60 members

Mayer Anselm Rothschild and Prince William IX

known as the "insinuators" whose mission was to affiliate others within the order, while keeping the true aims of the society secret. This involved enticing honest visionaries, rich people, society women, scientists, free thinkers, liberals, or any "enlightened" group that they could convince to further their interests. By 1786 there were lodges all over Europe, Africa, and America.

It was found that the best way to eliminate religion was to

April 1898 edition of Le Rire alluding to the global dominance of the House of Rothschild

split mankind into opposing ideologies and get them to fight amongst themselves, thus weakening national governments and organized religion. In 1781 Jews were allowed to join, and the Illuminati moved their headquarters to Frankfurt, where leading Jewish financiers were courted, including the Oppenheimers and the Rothschilds; since then the latter have become synonymous with the Illuminati and have now become the richest family in the world.

The Rothschilds empire was started in the 1750s by Mayer Amschel Rothschild, who dealt in rare coins and then moved into banking. He soon became court agent for Prince William IX of Hesse-Kassel, a nephew of the King of Denmark and the broker for big Frankfurt bankers. Prince William inherited his father's wealth in 1785 to become the richest individual in the world. The Rothschilds then made a killing during the Battle of Waterloo when early signs indicated that Napoleon would win. They sold all their stock on the English stock market with insider knowledge that Napoleon was about to be beaten. When stocks plummeted, they bought them cheap before news came through that Wellington had won. Now they effectively controlled the British economy and set up the Bank of England under Nathan Rothschild's control. They took control of the French economy in 1818 by buying vast quantities of French government bonds and then flooding the market. They also controlled the German money supply. They then appeared to finance both sides of every war since the American Revolution in the quest for one-world government (for example, during the Napoleonic wars, one branch of the family had financed Napoleon, the other Great Britain) and today are said to be behind the inevitable push towards a federal Europe.

Gordonstoun: an Illuminati school?

There are numerous universities and schools throughout the world that promote this agenda. Gordonstoun, attended by Prince Philip and the Prince of Wales, is alleged to be an Illuminati school. Perhaps the British Royal family are unwittingly serving the agenda of an Illuminati world order.

So, are they a bunch of evil puppet masters seeking world domination? Are they the power brokers behind the JFK assassination, the Federal Reserve, and the New World Order, or are they just a misunderstood bunch of Forbes rich-listers? Only time will tell.

Knights Templar

ROM THEIR FORMATION in 1118 with nine knights, this highly secretive order grew so rich and powerful over the course of the next two centuries that their wealth and land were second only to the Catholic church. Most controversially, they may have been in possession of religious or technological secrets that superseded the authority of the papacy. For these reasons they were crushed in 1307 by the pope and the French king. But during their ascendancy they became the forerunners of modern bankers and even invented the credit system.

Their tale begins in Jerusalem in 1118 when nine French knights gained permission from Jerusalem's King Baldwin II of Le Bourg to form a military order. Baldwin allowed them to live in the east wing of his palace, next to the ancient site where King Solomon's Temple had once stood.

They were known as the Order of the Poor Knights of Christ and the Temple of Solomon. Their leader was a French nobleman called Hugh de Payens—and they had close ties to the Cistercian monks, whose fortunes grew parallel with them. Ostensibly they formed to protect pilgrims journeying to the Holy Land. In practice their mission was entirely different.

They began excavating the site where Solomon's Temple had stood. Built 3,000 years ago, it was believed to have housed the Ark of the Covenant, the Hebrew's most sacred relic, said to be the portal through which they communicated directly with God. The temple was also thought to contain hidden knowledge older and more powerful than the Gospels. It is certain that the Templars built a system of underground passageways on the site—they were discovered by the British Royal Engineers at the end of the nineteenth century. What is less certain is the extent of the Templars' discoveries. Author Graham Hancock thinks it is unlikely that they found the Ark, since he believes that they would have returned to France triumphant (he makes a case for the Ark being hidden in Ethiopia). But it is very likely that they discovered powerful secrets ("sacred geometry") and scrolls about the life of Jesus that predate the Gospels and challenge orthodox views about the crucifixion and resurrection.

The Templars had a hierarchical structure (copied from the Cistercians and later adopted by the Freemasons) that consisted of knights, sergeants, chaplains, and servants. Originally the order required the vows of chastity and poverty. Anyone joining had to renounce his possessions and hand them over to the order. The Templars' power, wealth, and prestige increased rapidly. At their height they had 20,000 knights and a fearsome fighting reputation. They were easily recognizable in their white surcoats bearing a red cross.

In 1128 at the Council of Troyes, they were recognized by the Catholic church as an official military and religious order. Within a year they owned land throughout Europe, and in 1131 the King of Aragon gave them a third of his land. In 1139 Pope Innocent II granted them the right to answer only to the papacy, and they were also exempt from paying taxes, although they collected taxes for the church and the crown. They were also allowed to build their own churches. Thus they became the driving force behind some of the great medieval European churches, most notable Chartres Cathedral in Paris.

By spreading their influence and property, they became Europe's first bankers, in some cases charging up to 60 percent interest. They devised a credit arrangement whereby a pilgrim or merchant could deposit money or goods with them at one location in exchange for a promissory note, which he could cash in when he reached his destination. These early travellers' checks were an effective safeguard against tolls, church alms collectors, and thieves.

Graham Hancock is convinced that the Templars had "unearthed on the Temple Mount some repository of ancient knowledge concerning the science of building." This corresponds to a discovery made in 1947 on the shore of the Dead Sea. A "Copper Scroll" was found along with the Dead Sea Scrolls that mentions not only a horde of treasure—gold and writings—but also its location: Solomon's Temple. The idea of "sacred geometry" has often been thought of as the cornerstone of knowledge (and power) for secret mystery schools at a time when science, religion, and

victoriam non humane virtutis sed diuine gratie fateretur. In ea vastatione fuit ea hominū strages ea fa-
mes miserorꝫ funesta necessitas: Que si ex ordine noscere cupis Iosephum lege. Non audita sed visa et cō-
munia sibi cū ceteris referente. Uenies deuicꝫ Titꝰ romā cū patre suo Uespasiano triumphū celeberrimus
egit. Simone qui vrbis excidii causa fuit in triūpho pductū postea laqueo p totā ciuitate traxerunt multis
confossuꝫ vulneribꝰ interfecerūt. Uespasianꝰ templū pacis edificauit vbi iudeoꝛ preciosioꝛa instrumēta vt
delicet tabulas legis penetraliū vela. ꞇ alia multa reposuit. Ea aūt vrbs vsꝫ ad adriani principis tpa la-
tronū sicarioꝛūꝫ facta est receptaculū. ꞇ p quiquagita annos: deinde ciuitatis misere reliquit. Quā postea Adrianus impatoꝛ membꝰ ꞇ edificiis instaurans de suo noie heliam appellauit: et diuꝰ Hieronimꝰ ad
paulinū serit ꞇ ab adriani tpibus vsꝫ ad impium Constātini p annos circiter. clxxx. In loco resurrectiōis
simulacrū iouis in crucis rupe statua ex marmoꝛe veneris a gentilibꝰ posita colebaf. Estimātibꝰ psecutoꝛis
auctoꝛibꝰ ꝙ tolleret nobis fide resurrectiōis ꞇ crucis: si loca sancta p ydola polluissent. Maioꝛes dein nostri gloriosissimā ciuitatē diu possessā. tandē amiserūt. Karolus em magnꝰ multo sudoꝛe primo vrbē illaꝫ
vendicauit deinde pditam recupauit Gothofridus. Ad quā retinendā etiaꝫ Conradus cesar: Ludouicusꝫ
rex francoꝛ nō dubitarūt coactis exercitibꝰ in asiam pficisci. Et cū nri principes postea desidie sese dederūt
neꝫ hierosolima nec Antiochia in potestate nra remansere. Heu pudoꝛ: heu doloꝛ: fons ꞇ oꝛigo nre salutis
defecit. Templū illud Salomonis fama clarū: in quo dominꝰ tocies pdicauit: Bethlee in qua natꝰ est. Cal-
uariam in qua crucifixꝰ? Ipsius crucis possidēt inimici. Sepulcrus dni gloriosum in quo ꝓpter nos obꝛ-
muit in dno: saracenꝰ in prāte habet. ꞇt nisi velint xpiani imuisere nō possunt. En ipam dei viuētis ciuita-
tem officinasꝫ nre redēptiōis: quā dꝰ nr miraclis illustrauit ꞇ ꝓpꝛio sanguie dedicauit: In ꝗ pme resurre-
ctionis floꝛes apparuerīt: Machometi satellites occulcāt. Et ea vrbs nūc scelerate gentꝪ impio paret.

A medieval woodcut depicting Jerusalem

Quinta feculi etas Hic incipit et ortum habuit a captiuitate iudeorum in Babiloniam duratꝗſqꝫ ad christi iesu domini nostri natiuitatem per annos. 590. ꝗuis in hac supputatione aliqui aliter sentiant. Unde qui recte captiuitatis annos numerare voluerint ab vndecimo Sedechie regni anno vt Eusebius ponit. tunc septuaginta captiuitatis annos in secūdū Darij annū terminabunt . Joseph⁹ et diuus Dieronimus a.13. Josie regis vſqꝫ ad tercum Cyri regis annus. Monnulli ab vltimo regis Joachim anno computant vſqꝫ ad vltimum Cyri annum. At sane sentiendo septuaginta illi anni qui in tercio vel vltimo Cyri anno terminantur. propꝛie captiuitatis iudaice anni dicuntur. Illi vero qui in ſedo Darij terminantur propꝛie complete transmigrationis sunt. Et hec principaliot et precipua sacre scripture era habef .ꝗ.L.facta est anno ab eroꝛdio mūdi. 4 6 10. A diluuio aūt. 2 3 69. A natiuitate abrahe.1 4 2 7. Sic vigesi mooctauo regni Tarquini romanorum regis. Regnantibus etiam apud Medos astyage. apud Macedones Europe. Apudꝗ lydos alyacte: et apud egiptios vaphre: et apō Caldeos nabuchodonosoꝛ pmus .

Captiuitas igitur hebreorum que fuit exterminium populi hierusalē hic incipit. Et per annos. 70. perdurat. Cum enim populus israel iam multis temporibus ydolis seruiendo : etiam effusionem sanguinis innocentum se grauiter impiasset : volens deus generationem huius populi deperire : septuaginta annorum captiuitatem populum in regno caldeorum statui sustinere. Hac ratione vt completo annorum numero nouus populus a memoratis peccatis immunis ad renouationem hierusale perueniret.

magic were inseparable. Scientists today are no different from the ancient seekers and keepers of knowledge in that they search to reveal the hidden order to understand the mathematical relationships and harmonies that underlie the whole universe.

It is likely that the Templars' knowledge of sacred geometry accounts for why Chartres Cathedral was so vastly superior in design and technology to anything that had come before—pointed arches and high vaulted ceilings appeared for the first time—early Gothic architecture had arrived. Even the properties of the stained glass has never been successfully replicated by modern chemists.

The Templars achievements are plain to see, but it was their mania for secrecy that led detractors to believe that the Order of the Temple hid some dark secret. Their downfall was instigated in 1305 by France's King Philip IV, who convinced Pope Clement V that they were a threat to the papacy. It was also rumoured that the Templars intended to restore the Merovingian bloodline to the French throne. The Merovingians claimed descent from Jesus and that they were living proof that Jesus did not die on the cross.

On Friday, October 13, 1307, French authorities began capturing, interrogating, torturing, and burning Templars as heretics and blasphemers. As a climax to this inquisition, the last Grand Master, Jacques de Molay, was roasted to death in Paris in 1314. It marked the public end of a proud and secretive order.

But many questions still need answering. Much of the Templar's vast wealth remains unaccounted for, as does the Templar fleet— one of the largest of the time. Some researchers believe that it was the Templar treasure that François Bérenger Saunière discovered under the hilltop church of St. Mary Magdalene's in Rennes-le-Château (see the Priory of Sion, page 110).

Many of the Templars lived on—in fact only a small number were killed. Many escaped; some were even thought to have been pardoned by the Pope. They went underground, prompting claims that the Templars not only continued in secret, but that they survive to this day.

Ku Klux Klan

You will place your left hand over your heart and raise your right hand to heaven.

— OATH OF ALLEGIANCE —

SECTION 1.—OBEDIENCE

(You will say) "I" —— (Pronounce your full name —— and repeat after me) "In the presence of God and Man —— most solemnly pledge, promise and swear —— unconditionally —— that I will faithfully obey —— the constitution and laws —— and will willingly conform to —— all regulations, usages and requirements —— of the * * * * ——which do now exist —— or which may be hereafter enacted —— and will render at all times —— loyal respect and steadfast support —— to the Imperial Authority of same —— and will heartily heed —— all official mandates —— decrees —— edicts —— rulings and instructions —— of the I* W* thereof. —— I will yield prompt response —— to all summonses —— I having knowledge of same —— Providence alone preventing.

SECTION II.—SECRECY.

"I most solemnly swear —— that I will forever —— keep sacredly secret —— the signs, words and grip —— and any and all other —— matters and knowledge —— of the * * * * —— regarding which a most rigid secrecy —— must be maintained —— which may at any time —— be communicated to me —— and will never —— divulge same nor even cause same to be divulged —— to any person in the whole world —— unless I know positively —— that such person is a member of this Order —— in good and regular standing —— and not even then —— unless it be —— for the best interest of this Order.

"I most sacredly vow —— and most positively swear —— that I will never yield to bribe —— flattery —— threats —— passion —— punishment —— persecution —— persuasion —— nor any enticements whatever —— coming from or offered by —— any person or persons —— male or female —— for the purpose of —— obtaining from me —— a secret or secret information —— of the * * * * —— I will die rather than divulge same —— so help me God——

AMEN!''

You will drop your hands.

———————— O ————————

GENTLEMEN (or SIR):

You will wait in patience and peace until you are informed of the decision of the E* C* and his * in klonklave assembled.

———————— O ————————

(1

KKK members at cross-burning ceremony

T HE KU KLUX Klan's legacy of hatred and violence has its origins in the resentment of many white Southerners and Confederates after the Civil War. Having finally won the battle for freedom from slavery, blacks were confronted with the terror tactics of the Klan. In its heyday it attracted more than three million members, and though its fortunes have ebbed and flowed, it has never really disappeared.

The frontier spirit of an earlier era championed rugged individualism and the survival of the toughest. Along with this came frontier justice and vigilanteism. Before slavery was abolished, it was common practice (and legal) for groups of men to patrol their plantations and the surrounding area to prevent uprisings and whip any whom they caught breaking the curfew. This was followed by white Southerners' bitter defeat over slavery after a series of bloody slave revolts. The memory of these night posses formed a framework for subsequent Klan activities.

The Klan was dreamed up in the winter of 1865 by six young Confederate veterans in the small town of Pulaski, Tennessee. At first it was nothing more than a drinking club. They gave themselves silly names including the Grand Cyclops, Grand Magi, Grand Turk, and Grand Scribe, and members were to be called "ghouls." They chose a Greek word "kuklos" ("circle"), which sounded suitably mysterious, and then played around with alliteration and internal rhymes before settling on "Ku Klux Klan." The initials KKK would soon acquire a sinister significance throughout the United States.

At the same time it became clear that the Southern state legislatures would not relinquish power easily. They passed restrictive laws (which became known as the Black Codes) that all but reversed the blacks' hard-won freedom. Meanwhile President Andrew Johnson turned a blind eye to these retrogressive steps, but Congress showed its distaste for the Black Codes by refusing to seat Southern senators in December 1865. It seemed the Klan was ripe for hijacking by die-hard Southerners.

Their first night rides were irresponsible and childish pranks. They disguised themselves with sheets and caused quite a stir around the streets of Pulaski. They fashioned tall pointed hats and grotesque masks and adopted an initiation ceremony along the lines of a college fraternity, with ritual humiliation and silly oaths. But as their membership grew, the rides got out of hand. Black homes quickly became the primary targets for groups of white-sheeted riders threatening violence on blacks who didn't "behave" themselves. Threats turned into actual violence—whippings at first—and word quickly spread beyond Pulaski of a secret organization that was standing up for white freedom.

Within two years its membership had spread to Tennessee,

Alabama, Georgia, and Mississippi, and was in the thousands. Mass demonstrations could now take place and whole communities, black and white, could be intimidated with ease. In some counties the Klan had already become the invisible government with spies everywhere and, more importantly, influential members—editors, ministers, former Confederate officers, and political leaders. Vigilante justice was now being meted out to anyone who stepped out of line or threatened the organization.

At the time the Klan was being lead by General Nathan Bedford Forrest, a Confederate cavalry officer and the Klan's first Imperial Wizard. He travelled around the South opening up new cells and coordinating Klan activity.

During the summer of 1868 a rash of mutilations, floggings, lynching, and shootings spread across the South and degenerated into general lawlessness, with some Klan groups fighting each other. Congress was also on their case, so Forrest officially disbanded the Klan in January 1869 to absolve himself, but that didn't stop the violence, even though legislatures across the South were now imposing strict laws against Klansmen.

In 1871 Congress effectively banned the Klan—night riding and the wearing of masks were made illegal—and the president had the power to declare marshal law in the Southern states. Many Klansmen were arrested, and a few were imprisoned. But the damage had already been done—the Southern Democrats won more elections as frightened black voters stayed away from the polls, and they introduced a system of segregation—the "separate but equal" policy that held sway for the next 80 years.

The Klan went silent until its rebirth in the twentieth century. In the interim the country saw the influx of 23 million immigrants from Europe, the segregation laws kept on coming, and the 1890s witnessed a series of lynching of blacks by white mobs. But it wasn't until 1915, when a preacher-salesman William J. Simmons burned a cross in front of 15 fellow resurrected Klansmen at Stone Mountain, that the Klan became a formal movement again. His main aim was to make money, and although business was slow for several years, once he teamed up with publicists Edward Young Clarke and Elizabeth Tyler in 1920, American fears about being swamped by immigrants were the ideal breeding grounds for his new associates' relaunched anti-black, anti-Jewish, anti-Catholic, anti-immorality brand of hatred and paranoia.

They struck gold. Within a year they had 100,000 members and the joining fee of $10 made them rich, while their members nationwide threw themselves enthusiastically into renewed beatings, tar-and-feather raids, mutilations, and lynching of anyone considered anti-American—including "loose women" and Communists.

With their new found wealth came several years of bitter in-fighting between the Klan leaders, coinciding with a damaging exposé in the *New York World* which resulted in a 1921 congressional inquiry, the only effect of which seems to have been unprecedented free publicity for the Klan, whose numbers swelled to three million over the next four years.

They also succeeded in getting Klansmen into political office—Texas Klansman Earl Mayfield became a senator in 1922, and Klan influence helped the appointment of governors in Georgia, Alabama, California, and Oregon.

But a series of public court cases between Klan chiefs tarnished their moralistic reputation, and by 1926 their fortunes waned again. The Klan continued to shrink during the Great Depression of the 1930s, but pockets remained where it was still very active. It was finally nailed in 1944 when the Internal Revenue Service bankrupted it by chasing $685,000 in back taxes.

An Atlanta doctor, Samuel Green, tried to resurrect it again in 1949, and there is currently an organization today that calls itself the Knights of the Ku Klux Klan on an affirmative action, "Equal Rights for All, Special Privileges for None" ticket, that was founded in Louisiana in 1956, but fortunately nothing compares to the KKK's reign of terror in the early part of the twentieth century.

Mafia

"THE MAFIA IS oppression, arrogance, greed, self-enrichment, power and, hegemony above and against all others. It is not an abstract concept, or a state of mind, or a literary term. . . . It is a criminal organization regulated by unwritten but iron and inexorable rules. . . . The myth of a courageous and generous 'man of honor' must be destroyed, because a mafioso is just the opposite."

These are the words of Cesare Terranova, Italian Magistrate, shortly before he was murdered by the mob in 1979.

The Italian Mafia is also known as La Cosa Nostra, which means "This Thing of Ours" or "Our Affair." It originated in Sicily as a mutual preservation and protection society (much like the Triads—see page 130) during the Spanish occupation of Sicily, although some sources trace it as far back as 1282 during a rebellion in Sicily against King Charles I, known as the Sicilian Vespers.

An alternative interpretation of the origin of the word "Mafia" also relates to this event. A Sicilian woman, discovering her young daughter being raped by a French soldier at Vespers (the start of evening prayer), ran through the streets of Palermo yelling "Ma Fia! Ma Fia!" The insurrection that followed lasted for six weeks and resulted in the massacre of a large number of Sicily's French population. A third explanation is "Morte Alla Francia Italia Anela" ("Death to the French is Italy's Cry").

The protective function of the Mafia was carried to the United States during the large influx of Italian immigrants at the end of the nineteenth and the first half of the twentieth centuries. Many Italians preferred to rely on their networks of vigilante justice rather than on the local police authorities, whom they considered corrupt (often with good reason).

Nowadays the Mafia's criminal activity is much more "white collar," hi-tech, and global, but in the early days extortion, loansharking, smuggling of alcohol during Prohibition (and later drugs), prostitution, and illegal gambling were their key opera-

John Gotti on his way to Appeals Court

tions (it was the Mafia who turned Las Vegas into the gambling mecca of the world).

The Mafia has been spread throughout all the regions of Italy for hundreds of years, each network and family (or corsche—clans in Sicily) specific to the locality. For instance, the Mafia in Naples is called the Camorra; in Apulia it is known as the Sacra corona unita. It is also suspected that some of the key Mafia leaders during the inter-war Fascist years in Italy were active in the Fascist militia, but many also fled the country and fought against Mussolini.

Of those that settled in the United States, the mob in Chicago flourished with the activities of Al Capone ("Scarface"), although by the early 1900s there was a Mafia presence in every large city in the United States. In 1931 Capone was imprisoned in Alcatraz for income tax evasion, so the Mafia focused on New York, where five families rose to prominence:

the Bonanno family, the Colombo family, the Gambino family, the Genovese family, and the Lucchese family.

Like any secret society it has initiation rites, which are thought to involve the burning of a picture of a Catholic saint that has been smeared with drops of blood from the initiate's finger. An initiate would be known as a "made man." Before being offered membership he would have been observed for a long time and would have had to prove his criminal calibre. He would then become a Sgarrista (foot soldier) and would be given instructions passed down through several levels of the Mafia hierarchy—this protected those higher up the chain, especially the Capo Crimini (the "boss"; the term "Godfather" has also passed into folklore since Francis Ford Coppola's trilogy of films in the 1970s) and his right-hand man who was known as the consigliere ("counselor").

They also operated a strict code of silence called Omertà ("manhood"), which meant that anyone arrested by the authorities would never implicate or name anyone else in the organization. Anyone who broke the code would be assassinated, while those who acted with honour and kept quiet would ensure that his family was well looked after during his imprisonment. The concept of a vendetta is also a central part of the Mafia code. Loyalty to the mob was everything. You join on your feet and you leave in a coffin.

It would be many years before this code was broken. Joe Valachi of the Genovese family was the first Mafia member to break Omertà. In October 1963 he gave evidence to a congressional committee that acknowledged the Mafia's existence. This had a huge impact on the mob that was unrivalled until the 1990s when notorious mobster John Gotti was arrested by the FBI and charged with murder, drug smuggling, and extortion. His underboss Salvatore "Sammy the bull" Gravano turned states evidence and then disappeared into the Witness Protection program. Previously Gotti had been nicknamed the "Teflon Don" because of three separate trials in the 1980s that had fallen apart under mob pressure and resulted in his acquittal.

Majestic-12,

The Aviary, and

The Aquarium

RELEASED IN 1987, several top secret intelligence memos today continue to cause controversy in the UFOlogy community. Some believe they are fraudulent; others see them as evidence that the United States military recovered bodies and an alien spacecraft near Roswell, New Mexico, in July 1947 and that a secret group, known as Majestic-12, was formed to hide the fact that our planet is not the only one in the universe harbouring intelligent life.

These Majestic-12 documents were leaked by UFOlogist William L. Moore. One is a memo dated September 24, 1947, from President Truman to Defense Secretary James Forrestal, authorizing the creation of the group (see www.mufor.org/majic/majic6.jpg); the second, dated November 18, 1952, was a preliminary briefing to President-elect Eisenhower from Rear Admiral R.H. Hillenkoetter, who had been the director of the CIA, listing the members of Majestic-12 (see www.mufor.org/majic/majic2.jpg); the third dated July 13, 1953, was from Special Assistant to the President Robert Cutler to United States Air Force Chief of Staff General Nathan Twining (see www.mufor.org/majic/majic7.jpg).

The UFOlogy community is divided over the authenticity of these documents, but there are three possibilities:

- they and the MJ-12 were made up by Moore
- the MJ-12 exists but the documents were fakes intended to flush out the real members of the MJ-12
- both the MJ-12 and the documents are genuine

In the early 1970s, a group of approximately a dozen individuals with very high security clearances came together unofficially, and secretly, to pool their findings about extra terrestrial visitation and UFOs. According to Researcher Richard J. Boylan, Ph.D., "Their objectives were to coordinate data, see the big picture, analyze the meaning of UFOs and extraterrestrial contact with Earth, use this knowledge to gain access to additional information on the hyper secret Majestic-12 . . . and gain special influence through their collective power."

All these men were high ranking figures in intelligence and/or the United States military and were involved in UFO research and policy making. They gave themselves code names, using the names of birds, so the group became known as the Aviary. It then began leaking classified information to the general public in order to ease them in gently to the idea that extraterrestrials

were a reality. There seems to have been overlap between the members of the Aviary and the Majestic-12 group, but it is unclear if the latter infiltrated the Aviary to control it, spread misinformation, and disrupt their activities. It is believed that a split developed within the group, with some members seeking greater disclosure and candour, with the other faction wanting to be more cautious about making such shocking revelations public.

Another leak said to have originated with the Aviary are photographs of pages from a secret government manual on the procedures to follow when recovering crashed UFOs. This manual, dated April 1954 and entitled "Extraterrestrial Entities and Technology Recovery and Disposal," was received on a roll of 35mm film by UFO researcher Don Berliner.

All these documents have been scrutinized and debated for decades by UFOlogists, but many who think the documents are

A weather balloon was used as a cover-up for the Roswell incident fakes still believe in the existence of Majestic-12 and that they may be part of an elaborate misinformation campaign.

Dr. Steven Greer, Director of CSETI (Center for the Search for Extraterrestrial Intelligence) has reported that the MJ-12 has been recoded as PI-40 and is now so classified that the president and Congress have little knowledge of and no control over it, despite the possibility that millions of dollars of government money are illegally disappearing into this "black arm" of the United States military.

But a group even more obscure than the Aviary and the MJ-12, called the Aquarium, is said to have been created by the Aviary "to prepare human consciousness for the 'Eschaton' or spiritual emergency preceding the end of the world. The Aquarium is thought to be working to shift human consciousness with regard to NHI (non-human intelligence)."

In "The Aquarium Conspiracy," a memo spread around computer bulletin board systems in the spring of 1993, Dan Smith and Rosemary Ellen Guiley, directors of the Center for North American Crop Circle Studies, warned of an "eschatological emergency" and claimed, "The Aviary functions best by amplifying people's own misconceptions . . . by helping to overinflate individual pieces of the puzzle so that particular investigators get pushed further into their own blind alleys. . . . This cacophony by people looking for truth in all the strangest places provides an excellent cover for the deadly serious business of clearing the decks and battening down the hatches for the eschaton event."

It may be impossible to pin down the truth behind the Majestic-12 documents, but many UFOlogists from both sides of the debate concerning their authenticity, believe that the Majestic-12, the Aviary, and the Aquarium did exist and still do, albeit in more classified and modified forms.

If the truth is out there, it is likely to be hiding behind the lies and misinformation that continue to leak from these top secret groups. If the MJ-12 documents seem too good to be true, maybe the truth is too shocking to be revealed.

Mensur

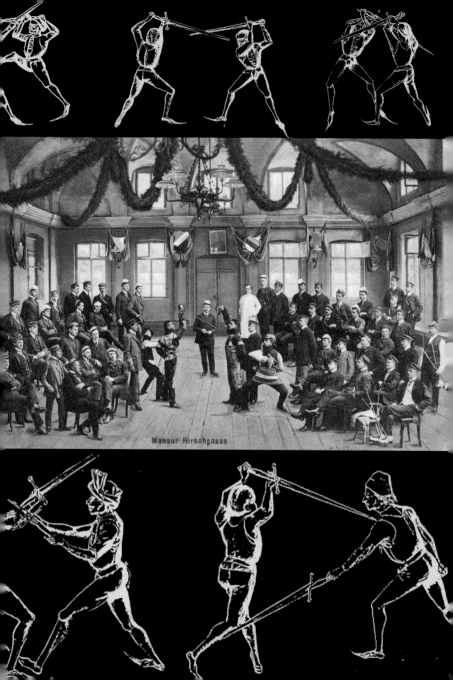

Mensur Hirschgasse

IN THE FIFTEENTH century, German students travelled in groups to protect themselves from bandit attacks. They were duellists, skilled in fencing, and there was strength in numbers. The students formed clubs that fought each other within a strict code of conduct, which elevated honour, loyalty, bravery, and fair play above all other virtues. But their story doesn't stop five centuries ago: these clubs still exist. They are highly secretive and their membership is usually taken from Germany's upper classes. They are called the Mensur.

Currently there are thought to be 200 student corps in Germany. They are shunned by many Germans who view them as neo-Nazis, but the alumni are in positions of power in German society, well-placed to pull strings for the young members now passing through the ranks.

Each fuchs (fox—a pledge, or freshman member, of a duelling fraternity who has not yet fought a sharp) must perform three mensur, or duels, before becoming a full member. Duellists wear black steel goggles and nose guards, and a thick binding is worn around the neck to protect the carotid artery. A chain mail shirt and gloves complete their bizarre and antiquated "protection" against the schalger, a rapier-like sword with a razor-sharp blade.

Two duellists stand face to face, at sword's length apart, with the sole aim of slashing his opponent's face above the eyeline, while maintaining a stoical expression, totally devoid of emotion. Any display of fear brings shame and defeat.

A silent wall of members surrounds them, drinking and smoking while watching the proceedings. Some of them bear the scars of previous duels—a sign of breeding and courage.

Suddenly, there is a barked order to raise swords. A brief, taut silence is followed by the command to commence battle. Weapons strafe together in a lightning quick succession of delicate yet lethal movements, attacks, and counter attacks cascading faster than the blink of an eye. The naked aggression of the dance of blades is in sharp contrast to the blank faces of the duellists, who stand immobile, their left hands tightly clasping the belt behind their backs. Another barked order cuts

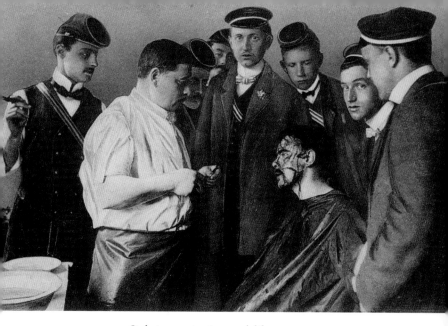

Student surgeon treating wounded fencer

into the cantata of clashing foils and then, as suddenly as they began, the fighters cease and lower their blades in a sideways arc. The drawing of blood has brought the duel to its conclusion.

When a man is cut, a student doctor applies surgical spirit and stitches up the wound on the spot, without anaesthetic, and the combatant will be scarred for life with a schmiss—the mark of nobility that will gain him advancement from other "brothers" for the rest of his privileged life.

Their loyalty is such that Adolf Hitler actually banned the corps because they would not split from their Jewish corps "brothers." Outsiders still see them as a group of dangerous right-wingers, others as an obsolete aristocratic curiosity, but every year in universities all over the country, new members secretly join or are invited as sons of old boys, attracted by the camaraderie, code of honour, the chances of advancement, and maybe, above all, the desire to master their bodily fear and explore complex animal instincts deep within.

Opus Dei

DEEP WITHIN THE Catholic Church is a secretive and elitist sect that only recently came to wider public attention. It is an organization that has the blessing of the pope, and it is accountable only to the Vatican (the pope gave it "personal prelature" status in 1982). You don't go looking for it. You don't have to. If you are a young and devout Catholic with a strong vocation, it comes looking for you.

The Opus Dei (God's Work) was founded in 1928 by Spanish priest Josemaría Escrivá. Its aim was to "spread throughout society a profound awareness of the universal call to holiness and apostolate through one's professional work carried out with freedom and personal responsibility." But despite its seemingly lofty intentions, Opus Dei has caused worldwide controversy for its bizarre and dictatorial practices, its enormous wealth, and the personality cult that seems to focus so much of its spiritual energy towards its founder rather than God.

Each year more and more ex-members are going public with their personal experiences of coercion and manipulation, being cut off from family and friends, having their intellectual freedom denied, enduring mortifications, complete obedience to flawed superiors, and facing eternal damnation when they tried to break free.

To a devout Catholic the message of the Opus Dei is very compelling: through devotion to the sect one can become a saint in one's everyday life. A prospective new recruit is targeted by an Opus Dei numerary and befriended. In fact, recruitment is the top priority. At any time each numerary has a list of 10 to 15 candidates that he or she is seeking to befriend and recruit. They keep secret dossiers on these so-called friends, and report back each week to superiors about his or her progress. The numerary's most powerful mind-control weapon is known in religious circles as the vocation trap. A potential new recruit is given persuasive evidence of their vocation and that they have been chosen by God. By the time this vocation has been acknowledged by the recruit, he or she will already have invested so much emotional commitment that to turn away feels like a mortal sin.

Once recruited, a numerary becomes essentially a plainclothed monk or nun, observing both celibacy and poverty. If they are working, they must give all their salary to the Opus Dei. For two hours each day, they must wear a spiked chain called a cilice around the upper thigh, which is very painful and leaves small prick holes in the flesh. They must also use a cordlike whip on their buttocks and back once a week and suffer other more minor mortifications such as sleeping on the floor or fasting. Taken in isolation, this may seem misguided but not necessarily dangerous. But in the wider context of the Opus Dei's objectives, it is primarily a strong control mechanism, designed to subvert sexuality (authoritarian regimes always target the sexual urge as a means of control). It is even more worrying that the founder was allegedly a misogynist who believed that women had passions that required more discipline to tame.

The Opus's obsession with restraint of intellectual freedom is deeply disturbing. As critic Franz Schaefer so neatly puts it, "In the dictatorship-like structure of the Opus a mistake or an evil decision by just one person on top of the organization can have fatal consequences. Their response is something like: 'Oh well we have built a dictatorship, but do not be worried: we have such a nice dictator on top who is such a kind person with a good heart . . .' "

So, what sort of man was founder Josemaría Escrivá? In April 1990, Opus Dei priests presented Pope John Paul II information in support of Escrivá's beatification and canonization that led the pope to describe him as "heroically virtuous" (although unprecedented secrecy has prevented outsiders from seeing the evidence upon which this dubious assessment was based). In July of the following year, a miraculous healing attributed to Escrivá's intercession was authenticated, in part, by Opus Dei doctors (before a person can be canonized, evidence of miracles must be associated with the candidate).

Several ranking cardinals, at least one of the pope's personal secretaries, and key members of the pope's media relations team are Opus Dei members. So it is little wonder that Escrivá's canonization went so smoothly and any unsavoury details about his private life have been buried. Now this highly lucrative personality cult has a full-fledged saint to worship—powerful incentive indeed for an organization whose main message is "You too can become a saint," (so long as you give us all your money, punish yourself daily, obey completely, and stop thinking).

Reports from eyewitnesses who knew Escrivá, many of them women, show that he was far from saintly. In fact, he regularly failed to meet the normally accepted levels of human decency.

The beatification of Cardinal Escrivá

Former high-ranking Opus Dei member Maria Del Carmen Tapia has described him as vain, inconsistent, and, on occasion, obscenely angry. In her book, *Beyond the Threshold: Life in Opus Dei*, she describes his reaction to the discovery that a woman had helped her to secretly mail letters. He angrily shouted the woman's punishment: "Draw up her skirts, tear down her panties and give it to her in the ass!" This alone should have been enough to scrap his chances of becoming a saint, but this and many other eyewitness accounts have been brushed aside and discredited by high-ranking Opus Dei leaders.

This urge to control information to acquire and maintain power runs throughout the strictly hierarchical structure of the Opus Dei. Absolute obedience to authority is paramount. A key text is Escrivá's book *The Way*, which is laced with the theme of blind obedience without stopping to consider the reasons, is trusting that one will not be directed to do anything that is not good and "for the glory of God." Chapter 2, "Guidance," repeatedly rams home the message of obedience to an authoritarian "Director" (he is not referring to God).

Incoming and outgoing private mail of members is read and censored. Members are forbidden from reading anything without first getting permission from their spiritual directors, even if they are required reading for a university course. The directors keep an extensive list of banned books. Furthermore, a former numerary, Joseph Gonzales, claims, "I witnessed the numeraries, including the directors, intermittently burning books in the garden at the back of the center. Usually Protestant Bibles and books on the theory of evolution." He also describes being subjected to "psychological coercion," the "misconstruction of vocation," and "stigmatization" when "the directors represented leaving Opus Dei as a mortal sin."

In an interview with GQ magazine in December 2003, Sharon Clasen, recruited as a freshman at Boston College in 1981, describes how she was cut off from her family ("Opus Dei was her family now," she was told). She endured all the punishments described above, and when she tried to leave, she was threatened with damnation to hell. The only photos she was allowed to possess were of Josemaría Escrivá.

There are 85,000 Opus members worldwide. In the United States there are just 3,000, but as the GQ article points out, "Some of the country's best-known conservatives have been pegged as Opus Dei sympathizers or friends: Antonin Scalis, Clarence Thomas, Robert Bork, Republican senators Rick Santorum and Sam Brownback, former Information Awareness Office director John M. Poindexter and TV pundits Lawrence Kudlow and Robert Novak."

This "Holy Mafia" continues to destroy lives and control minds while amassing ever more power and wealth. It has recently built a $47 million lavish headquarters in the centre of Manhattan. The founder's photographs appear everywhere. A visitor would be hard pressed to interpret the entire edifice as anything less than a worldly manifestation of the personality cult of "Saint" Josemaría Escrivá.

The Order of Skull and Bones

Ⓨ ALE IS THE top university in the United States. The annual tuition fees are $28,400, which excludes all but the most privileged or most intellectually gifted (with scholarships) from attending. The fact, therefore, that Yale alumni fill positions of power is inevitable and well known, but there is a secret Yale club which can propel the elite within that elite to the most powerful positions in the world, including key positions within the CIA and the top job—president of the United States. Many believe it is the American branch of the Illuminati (see page 62). The name of the club is the Skull and Bones.

George W. Bush, a "C" grade student from one of the most highly placed families in the world, attended Yale in the 1960s and, like his father George H.W. Bush, joined the Skull and Bones. For a man with such undeniably modest abilities, he has truly reached a pinnacle of power that only money and influence can buy. The fact that his presidential opponent in 2004, John Kerry, also attended Yale is not surprising. That he should also have been a member of the Skull and Bones is too close for comfort.

Yale's famous benefactor, Elihu Yale, was born near Boston, Massachusetts, on April 5, 1649. Educated in London, he made

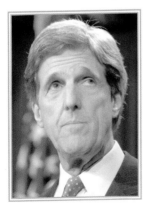

Kerry: Skull and Bones member

his fortune in the British East India Company and later became governor of Fort St. George in India, an important trading post and centre of diplomacy. After several bequests, Yale College was named after him in 1718. Nearly 60 years later, a 21-year-old Yale graduate member of the "Culper Ring," America's first intelligence operation, was hanged in New York and became a martyr of the American Revolution. There is a statue of him on Yale's Old Campus. Ever since, Yale has had a unique rela-

SECRET SOCIETIES AT YALE COLLEGE.—[FROM A DRAWING BY MISS ALICE DONLEVY.]

The secret societies of Yale University

tionship with United States intelligence, and now the CIA (a statue of Yale stands outside the CIA's headquarters in Langley, Virginia). Apparently there were so many Yale graduates in the Office of Strategic Services (or OSS, the forerunner of the CIA), that Yale's drinking tune, the "Whiffenpoof Song," didn't just echo around the neo-Gothic quadrangles of the University, but soon became the unofficial anthem of the OSS.

The Skull and Bones story begins in 1832 when William H. Russell (whose family had made its fortune smuggling Turkish opium to China) and 14 other Yale undergraduates became its founding members. Russell had studied in Germany the year before. According to details stolen from the Skull and Bones in

1876 by a group calling itself The Order of File and Claw, "Bones is a chapter of a corps in a German University. . . . General Russell, its founder, was in Germany before his Senior Year and formed a warm friendship with a leading member of a German society. He brought back with him to college, authority to found a chapter here." Many researchers believe the German society mentioned to be the Illuminati, which shares the skull and bones as its official emblem; Ron Rosenbaum claims the two groups have many ritualistic elements in common.

The "tomb"

Every year since then, 15 juniors are "tapped" by the seniors to be initiated. The family names on the Skull and Bones roster read like an elite country club list: Taft, Jay, Bundy, Rockefeller, Goodyear, Sloane, Stimson, Phelps, Perkins, Pillsbury, Kellogg, Vanderbilt, Bush, Lovett. From 1856 they have met to perform their arcane initiation rites in the "tomb," a vine-covered, windowless hall on campus. It is also thought that each initiate is given a substantial sum of money as a springboard to post-collegiate success (although this is more an indication of the wealth of the Russell Trust which funds the Order, since none of the wealthy Bonesmen could claim to be short of money).

Fifty years after the Order's founding, in October of 1873, Volume 1, Number 1, the first and only issue of *The Iconoclast* spoke out in criticism of Skull and Bones:

"Out of every class Skull and Bones takes its men. They have gone out into the world and have become, in many instances, leaders in society. They have obtained control of Yale. Its business is performed by them. Money paid to the college must pass into their hands, and be subject to their will. No doubt they are worthy men in themselves, but the many, whom they looked down upon while in college, cannot so far forget as to give money freely into their hands. Men in Wall Street complain that the college comes straight to them for help, instead of asking each graduate for his share . . . Year by year the deadly evil is growing. The society was never as obnoxious to the college as it is today, and it is just this ill-feeling that shuts the pockets of non-members. Never before has it shown such arrogance and self-fancied superiority. It grasps the College Press and endeavors to rule it all. It does not deign to show its credentials, but clutches at power with the silence of conscious guilt. . . . To tell the good which Yale College has done would be well nigh impossible. To tell the good she might do would be yet more difficult. The question, then, is reduced to this—on the one hand lies a source of incalculable good—on the other a society guilty of serious and far-reaching crimes. It is Yale College against Skull and Bones!! We ask all men, as a question of right, which should be allowed to live?"

Russell's family wasn't unique in becoming wealthy from the opium trade. In fact, drugs, oil, warfare, and weapons have built and consolidated the power bases of all American and European dynasties. All warfare since then has been a direct application of Hegel's dialectic principles—thesis pitted against antithesis to safeguard and increase this wealth and power and ultimately to bring about a New World Order.

Some would argue further that globalization, materialism, and the permissive society is another way that the Bonesmen are successfully ushering in a New World Order by breaking down the family unit—the single biggest obstacle to totalitarian mind control—while being seen publicly to be struggling to protect it. The most visible and vocal protectors of morality are the very people who are working behind the scenes to destroy it.

The Priory of Sion

(Sionus Prioratus)

*T*HE STORY OF the Priory of Sion is a saga that leapfrogs around a time frame of nearly a thousand years and is a confusing network of intertwining mysteries, of French nobles, Belgian monks, Frankish kings, the Turin Shroud, secret codes, the Catholic Church, and an allegedly unbroken line of original thinkers, occultists, and alchemists. The Priory of Sion may in truth be the guardians of political, religious, and esoteric secrets so powerful that they could destroy nations and the central tenet of the Christian Church.

The secret society was formed in 1090 by Godfroi de Bouillon, a French nobleman who was one of the leaders of the First Crusade and was offered the position of king of Jersualem—a title which he refused, accepting instead the Defender of the Holy Sepulchre. He had travelled to Jerusalem with a conclave of Belgian monks who believed that he was descended from the Merovingians, a dynasty of Frankish kings.

The Merovingians had ruled over a substantial part of what has now become France between the fifth and seventh centuries, but they were overthrown by the rival Carolinian dynasty. History records that the dynasty died out at this point, but the *Dossiers Secrets* (a collection of Priory of Sion documents, deposited anonymously in the Bibliothèque Nationale in Paris during the 1960s) asserts that it has survived owing to its secret activities.

The Priory of Sion also claims to have influenced many world events in an attempt to restore descendants of the Merovingian bloodline into political power through a network of secret, esoteric, and occult practices. Many of its Grand Masters were alchemists or occultists and have been behind various esoteric groups such as the Rosicrucians (see page 118) and some orders of Freemasons (see page 46).

The society's first base was the Abbey of Our Lady of Mount Sion in Jerusalem, the building of which was ordered by Godfroi de Bouillon. The knights attached to it called themselves the Knights of the Order of Our Lady of Sion, and at this early stage they appear to have been associated with the Knights Templar (see page 68), but they parted company with each other in 1188.

The first Grand Master (or *Nautonnier*) was a Norman nobleman named Jean de Gisors. Subsequent Grand Masters have adopted the name Jean (or Jeanne for a woman). These have included Sandro Botticelli, Leonardo Da Vinci, Nostradamus, Isaac Newton, Victor Hugo, Claude Debussy, and Jean Cocteau. The current Grand Master is rumoured to be a Spanish lawyer and the name Pablo Norberto has been circulated, but this individual remains unidentified. Others believe the incumbent lives in Belgium.

If the story ended there, it would be merely a curiosity, an esoteric diversion, possibly even an elaborate and well-researched hoax, but there are other threads woven into the complex fabric of this extraordinary tapestry.

In the 1990s British researchers Lynn Picknett and Clive Prince were working on the Turin Shroud when they were approached by an individual who claimed to be a member of the Priory of Sion. He offered them inside information that the Turin Shroud had been faked in 1492 by the twelfth Grand Master, Leonardo da Vinci, using his own face and "alchemical imprinting"—a crude photographic technique. Picknett and Prince followed up the claim with their own research and in 1994 published *Turin Shroud: In Whose Image? The Truth Behind the Centuries-Long Conspiracy of Silence,* and three years later, *The Templar Revelation: Secret Guardians of the True Identity of Christ.*

Another strand appeared with the discovery by a 33-year-old priest in a small Catholic church in 1885. The priest was François

Bérenger Saunière, and his discovery was made in the hilltop church of St. Mary Magdalene in the tiny parish of Rennes-le-Château. The church, in the Languedoc region of France, had originally been the private chapel of the lords of Rennes-le-Château.

In 1891, while restoring the church, Saunière discovered a secret parchment inside one of the ancient altar supports, which some accounts report as dating back to the Visigothic period of the seventh or eighth century. Other accounts claim that he found four separate documents—two genealogies dating from 1244 and 1644 and two letters. He also discovered two encrypted messages in the graveyard outside on the tombstone of Marie de Nègre d'Ables, Lady of Blanchfort, and the last Lord of Rennes-le-Château, who had died in 1781.

He took his findings to his superior, the Bishop at Carcassonne, who sent him to Paris to the Saint Sulpice Seminary (a place that is thought to have been the headquarters of a secret society called the Compagnie du Saint-Sacrement, an early incarnation of the Priory of Sion).

While Saunière was in Paris, he began moving in elite circles, and may even have had an affair with a Parisian opera singer named Emma Calve, who was a high-ranking occultist (she visited him frequently at Rennes-le-Château). Whatever the nature of this relationship, one thing is certain: after his return from Paris, Saunière experienced a dramatic change in his fortunes. He received vast sums of money to refurbish the church and to build many other structures in the area, including an extensive library, a zoological garden, and a round tower called Tour Magdala (Tower of Magdalene—the woman from whom the Merovingians claim descent as the mother of Jesus' children). He also commissioned a statue of Asmodeus ("destroyer"), the name of the apocalyptic and sexually deviant demon mentioned in the Old Testament's Book of Tobias (iii, 8) , and a powerful occult figure and the mythological builder of Solomon's Temple. Asmodeus is also the symbol for anarchy—an upper case "A" inside a circle is a depiction of Asmodeus.

Inside the church, Saunière built a painted panel which is an ambiguous depiction of the body of Jesus being carried to the tomb, although the scene takes place under a full moon, and can be interpreted as the moment when his body was secretly *removed* from the tomb at night. He erected a plaque over the church entrance which read, *Terribilis Est Locus Iste* ("This place is terrible"), which is strikingly similar to Jacob's exclamation in Genesis 28:17 when he saw the Gate of Heaven.

His windfall, and subsequent ostentatious wealth, coincides precisely with his important findings. He was defrocked in 1912 and died five years later in mysterious circumstances. He suffered a stroke five days after his housekeeper Marie Dernaud had ordered a coffin for him, and when a priest heard his confession, he refused to give Saunière the last rites. The secret of his wealth was apparently entrusted to his housekeeper, who said she would reveal it on her deathbed. Unfortunately she, too, suffered a stroke that left her paralyzed and unable to speak, so the secret died with her.

The two encrypted messages on the tombstone of Marie de Nègre d'Ables and the Lord of Rennes-le-Château read:

THIS TREASURE BELONGS TO DAGOBERT II
KING AND TO SION AND HE IS THERE DEAD.

and

SHEPHERDESS NO TEMPTATION THAT POUSSIN
TENIERS HOLD THE KEY PEACE 681 BY THE
CROSS AND THIS HORSE OF GOD I DESTROY
THIS
DAEMON GUARDIAN AT MIDDAY. BLUE APPLES.

The second message was decoded using a puzzle called the Knight's Tour of the Chessboard, in which the Knight travels to every square on the board once, combined with a cipher "MORT EPEE" taken from the Marie de Nègre tombstone. It is claimed that it refers to three paintings: Poussin's *Shepherds of Arcadia*,

Teniers' *Temptation of St. Anthony*, and a portrait of Pope Celestine V (who was the only Pope to resign). Saunière is supposed to have viewed all three paintings at the Louvre during his visit to Paris.

So what were Saunière's other links to the Priory of Sion? The answer lies in the symbolism that he incorporated into his decorated church, which is unusual by conventional Catholic standards and is open to Masonic interpretations. For example, French author Gérard de Sède argues that the ninth station of the cross relates to a Masonic order known as the Beneficent Knight of the Holy City. Saunière appears to be linked to Rectified Scottish Rite and also attended meetings of the Martinist Order in Lyons. Add the fact that the noble families of Rennes-le-Château were also Masonic, and it is very likely that Saunière's good fortune was also Masonic. According to Picknett and Prince, the "Priory of Sion" is really a "cover" used by members of the Rectified Scottish Rite and the Martinist Order.

In *The Jesus Conspiracy: The Turin Shroud and the Truth About the Resurrection*, Holger Kersten and Elmar R. Gruber claim that the Catholic Church engineered the Turin Shroud's exposure as a fake, because the truth would destroy the church. They reached the shocking conclusion that Jesus was alive when he was covered by the shroud and placed in his tomb. The authors Michael Baigent, Richard Leigh, and Henry Lincoln reached a similar conclusion in their best sellers *The Holy Blood and the Holy Grail* and *The Messianic Legacy*, that Jesus did not die on the cross, but lived to marry and father children with Mary Magdalene, whose descendants are the Merovingians.

Is this the Masonic secret that made Saunière rich? That Jesus was not resurrected, because he didn't die on the cross; that the Holy Grail isn't a cup, but is symbolic of the Merovingian blood line which lives on—a secret so dangerous that whoever discovers it must enter a Faustian pact and accept earthly treasures in exchange for silence?

The Rosicrucians

HE ROSICRUCIANS DEVELOPED from various groups of
alchemists, Christian Kabbalists, and rational humanists
who came together in the 1500s to form a blend of mystical Christianity and enlightenment scholarship. One such figure,
Dr. John Dee, wrote a tract called *Monas Hieroglyphica* and travelled through Europe spreading its teachings.

This group of like-minded free-thinkers began calling themselves Rosicrucians around this time, although it would be
another century before they came into public notice. The
Moravian alchemist Michael Sendivogius' Society of the
Unknown Philosophers is believed to be a forerunner of the
movement. In 1604 he published his manuscript, *Twelve Treatises
on the Philosophers' Stone*, and had already made a name for
himself with a mysterious powder that he had acquired from
Alexander Seton, another alchemist whom he had rescued from
imprisonment by Christian II of Saxony.

The fraternity was made public with the 1614 publication of three
manuscripts in Germany by Lutheran theologian Johann Valentin
Andreae (though some attribute it to Sir Francis Bacon, a senior figure in the order). The first was the *Fama Fraternitas,* which talked of
an "invisible college" of enlightened men and set out the aims of
the order. It is likely that Andreae, like many of his contemporaries,
was inspired by the ideas and courage of the mathematician and
Neo-Platonic mystic, Giordano Bruno—a genius statistician, tor-
tured by the Church before being burned as a heretic in 1600.

Fama Fraternitas also told the allegory of Christian Rosencreuz
(Rosy-cross), a poor but noble knight who was born in Germany
in 1358. He had learned alchemical secrets in Arabia before
returning to his native Germany, where he formed a lodge called
the House of the Holy Spirit with eight disciples. The number
eight has a mystical significance for the order, expressed in their
symbol of a pelican ripping open its breast to feed its seven
dependants. These founder members developed a secret language

and compiled a book of alchemical wisdom. Their mission was to "learn to know all, but keep *thyself* unknown." They lived their life by six rules:

1. To make no public profession of superior knowledge, and to heal the sick free of charge.
2. To wear no special garment, but to dress according to the custom of the country in which they lived.
3. To return to the House of the Holy Spirit on a certain day each year, for the purpose of mutual help and instruction.
4. To seek a worthy person to succeed each member.
5. To adopt the letters R.C. as their sign and mark.
6. To keep the existence of the fraternity a secret for a period of 100 years.

The publication of *Fama Fraternitas* was followed in 1615 by *Confessio Fraternitatis* and *Chemische Hochzeit Christiani Rosenkreuz 1459 (Chymical Marriage of Christian Rosenkreutz)* in 1616. All three manifestos created a sensation among European intellectuals, scientists, and aristocracy in their quests for spiritual truth and personal enlightenment. Indeed, Rosicrucian ideas feel very modern and would not be out of place in this Age of Aquarius.

The rose had always been an alchemical symbol of spiritual transformation, and the cross was a symbol of the material world and of salvation. When these two symbols were combined it represented a gateway of spiritual awareness beyond the physical world. Some believe it was taken from the coat of arms of Martin Luther, although Andreae also used these symbols in his own coat of arms.

The secret burial vault of Rosencreuz was discovered in the House of the Holy Spirit 120 years after his death. Along with it were instructions to make the Rosicrucians' teachings known to the world, on condition that they should not be monopolized by any one Christian sect. The instructions invited men with pure hearts and sincere aspiration to approach the order, and warned off those with selfish motives.

The Rosicrucians were also known as the Fire-Philosophers.

They defined fire as "the most perfect and unadulterated reflection, in Heaven as on Earth, of the ONE FLAME. It is Life and Death, the origin and the end of every material thing. It is divine 'SUBSTANCE.' " One of their aims was to bring the disparate branches of occultism under one umbrella in the search for the invisible spirit in all matter. This ancient knowledge can be traced back to the mystery academies of ancient Egypt, founded by Pharaoh Thutmose III (1500–1477 B.C.), and to the Greek philosophers, such as Thales and Pythagoras. The Rosicrucians are reputed to have discovered the "eternal flame"—the secret of "ever-burning lamps" supposedly known to the ancients, which also relates to the secret of prolonging life.

In 1623 there were said to be only 36 Rosicrucians in Europe, scattered about in six different countries, though many prominent figures have been associated with them, including Leonardo da Vinci, Cornelius Heinrich Agrippa, Dante, René Descartes, Blaise Pascal, Isaac Newton, Gottfried Leibnitz, Christopher Wren, Benjamin Franklin (a Rosicrucian colony was established in Philadelphia in the seventeenth century), Thomas Jefferson, Michael Faraday, Claude Debussy, and Erik Satie.

Unlike other orders which sought to recruit and expand their membership, the Rosicrucians seem to have been genuinely more discreet and discerning. Allegiance was to one's true self and not to the order. Their secrecy seems to have been more about humility and the protection of knowledge from exploitation (and accusations of heresy) rather than to create a mystique or a false sense of importance. And while other secret orders and alchemists sought power and wealth (base metals into gold), they were seeking the correct "Way" as laid down in the Instructions in 1675. These instructions are prefaced with a warning against using them for selfish ends. The greatest treasures known to man are described as lying in a mountain in the centre of the world, which is an allegorical reference to guidance to the riches of the self within. Sadly, by the mid–eighteenth century the Masons, Rosicrucians, and other orders with professed Templar origins had become so entwined that it is hard for the modern historian to tell them apart.

Round Table

THE BRAINCHILD OF Cecil Rhodes, one of the godfathers of Neo-Platonic eugenics and population control aficionados, the Round Table appears on the surface to be an organization of elderly men who plan charity events, jumble sales, and old boys' reunions. A closer look at the history and the motivation of its founder suggests that it had a much more sinister mission.

Cecil Rhodes was born in 1853, the son of a vicar. In 1879 he went to South Africa to become a diamond prospector, and founded de Beers Consolidated Mines, Ltd. By 1891 de Beers controlled 90 percent of the world's diamond production, and Rhodes developed a vision of rich white supremacy, the legacy of which still keeps the nations of Africa in a constant state of intertribal war and poverty. But he didn't do it alone. His mentor, whom he met while an undergraduate at Oxford, was fine arts professor John Ruskin, the man credited with calling for education of the working man. In fact, this was merely part of his plan to create an expanded middle class, which would labour on behalf of the aristocracy. They could then control them behind the scenes in a form of legal slavery through banking and supplying credit. He was also a misanthrope, a pederast, and a passionate believer in a tightly- and centrally-controlled autocracy by an elite and enlightened ruling class aptly characterized in his own words: "My continual aim had been to show the eternal superiority of some men to others, sometimes even of one man to all others." This is the tradition established by Plato in his *Republic,* which calls for a ruling class of philosopher kings "with a powerful army to keep it in power and a society completely subordinate to the monolithic authority of the rulers."

Rhodes clearly set out his plans for world domination as early as 1877. Disillusioned with the inward-looking nature of English Freemasonry (he was by then already a Master Mason), he wrote his "Confession of Faith," stating, "I contend that we [the English] are the finest race in the world and that the more of the world we inhabit the better it is for the human race. Just fancy those parts that are at present inhabited by the most despicable specimens of human beings what an alteration there would be if they were brought under Anglo-Saxon influence. . . . At the present day I become a member of the Masonic order I see the wealth and power they possess . . . and I wonder that a large body of men can devote themselves to what at times appear the most ridiculous and absurd rites without an object and without an end. . . . Why should we not form a secret society with but one object, the furtherance of the British Empire and the bringing of the whole uncivilized world under British rule for the recovery of the United States for the making the Anglo-Saxon race but one Empire."

Empowered by his ever-growing wealth and his monopoly over the South African diamond fields, inspired by Malthusian eugenics and John Ruskin, financially backed by the Rothschild family, and fuelled by his racism, Rhodes continued to refine his ideas in the seven wills, which he wrote during his lifetime. After Rhodes' death, Freemason Lord Nathan Rothschild became the trustee of his entire estate and immediately appointed Freemason Lord Alfred Milner to recruit a group of young Freemasons from Oxford University and Tonybee Hall to become founder members of the Round Table. (Milner's view on the new world order is best summed up by his own words: "My patriotism knows no geographical but only racial limits. I am a British Race patriot.")

The name Round Table comes from the court of legendary British King Arthur (whose quest for the Holy Grail is intricately linked with Freemasonry and the Illuminati). Inevitably, the new society was Masonic in structure. It consisted of a pyramid hierarchy, with inner and outer circles of influence and knowledge, called the Circle of Initiates and the Association of Helpers, and a complex smoke screen of corporate trusts, institutions, and educational foundations that would challenge even the most scrupulous auditor.

The Rhodes' Scholarship is one such supposedly philanthropic scheme that hides a deeper and darker agenda. Rhodes stipulated in his will the formation of a foundation to provide funding for exceptional American scholars to study at Oxford University.

David Icke has called this scheme "the center of the Illuminati's manipulation of 'education'. The ratio of these 'Rhodes Scholars' who go back to their countries to enter positions of political, economic, and media power is enormous compared with the general student population. They act as Illuminati agents. The most famous Rhodes Scholar in the world today is Bill Clinton, the two-time president of the United States."

Bill Clinton is no stranger to the idea that an elite more powerful than government has a stranglehold on the world economy. He is a member of the Bilderberg Group, and his mentor at Harvard was none other than Professor Carroll Quigley, author of *Tragedy and Hope: A History of the World in Our Time,* one of the most important macro-historical analyses of the collectivist one-world society, tracing the incomprehensible power exercised by the Rothschilds, the Bank of England, J. P. Morgan, and the Rockefellers. By 1900, according to Dr. Quigley, "the influence of these business leaders was so great that the Morgan and Rockefeller groups acting together, or even Morgan acting alone, could have wrecked the economic system of the country." The book reveals who runs the establishment, how it controls the universities, how it influences the election of United States presidents, and the influence of Cecil Rhodes: "These purposes centered on his desire to federate the English-speaking peoples and to bring all the habitable portions of the world under their control. For this purpose Rhodes left part of his great fortune to found the Rhodes Scholarships at Oxford . . ."

At the end of World War I it became clear that the Round Table could best be extended by the creation of an umbrella organization called The Royal Institute of International Affairs (which, as shown on page 38, is the British branch of the Council on Foreign Relations).

Triads

ALTHOUGH MODERN CHINESE Triad groups have a reputation for being a highly dangerous and intimidating criminal organization akin to the Russian and Italian Mafias, their origins are ancient and more humanitarian. The first known Chinese secret society was called the *Chi Mei* (Red Eyebrows) formed to overthrow the oppressive Han dynasty that ruled China from 206 B.C. to A.D. 220. The name referred to their practice of painting their eyebrows red, like those of a demon, to intimidate their opponents. The name "triad" was used much later by British authorities in Hong Kong, referring to the triangular shape of the Chinese character for "secret society."

These early societies grew through clan, family, and local ties and were really networks of mutual preservation. They have since mutated into protection rackets and international criminality, although even today modern Triad societies perform charitable works alongside their more substantial underworld interests. Today there are believed to be more than 180,000 Triad members and about 60 separate Triad organizations worldwide, though most of them can really only trace their origins as far back as the anti-Qing dynasty societies that formed between 1644 and 1911. The most famous of these was the *Hung Mun* (Hung Society), which emerged from an amalgamation of five others in the late seventeenth century.

Legend tells that these anti-Qing rebels began with five Buddhist fighting monks (the Five Ancestors of the Triads) from the Siu Lam Monestary (also known as the Shaolin) in the Fukien province. They had been working in cooperation with the second Manchurian emperor Kiang Hsi until he began to persecute them, and finally burned down their monastery, forcing them into underground resistance. They adopted a symbol of a red triangle bearing the Chinese character *Hung* (the family name of the deposed Ming emperor), representing a sacred trinity of heaven, the earth, and man. *Mun* is the Chinese word for red. They also disguised their activities under the name the Heaven and Earth Society.

Triads being executed by Chinese police

The Qing dynasty ruthlessly attempted to eliminate them, but they developed secret languages, oaths, and means of communication. Their intense secrecy and fraternal loyalty ensured that some modern Triad societies can claim descent from this branch. According to Benny Meng and Richard Loewenhagen, Hung Mun is still highly active in Taiwan with "over 100,000 active members including professionals, military men, and intelligence officers," although "according to researchers and governmental authorities, there is no evidence that [it] is involved in criminal activity." They suggest that "Dr. Sun Yat Sen, the founding father of today's Republic of China and the man credited with the final overthrow of the Qing Dynasty, was himself a secret society leader" and that "Shang Kai Shek, the first president of the Republic of China, was also a secret society leader. Most political experts today agree that Shek owed his successful bid for the presidency to the political support of the Hung Muhn Society."

Another pro-Ming secret group, the White Lotus Society, made its name during the Qing dynasty in the notorious tax rebellion of impoverished settlers in the mountains between the Szechuan province and the Hubei and Shansi provinces in 1796. They were an early doomsday cult, in the sense that they held a strong millenarian belief that the end of the world was approaching.

However, the most powerful and sophisticated Triads have sprung up in the last 50 years. Of these the *Sun Yee On* is the largest. It is based, like so many Triad groups, in Hong Kong, but has more than 56,000 members worldwide, with United States operations based in New York, Miami, San Francisco, and Los Angeles. The next largest is the 14K Triad with more than 20,000 members, most of Cantonese origin. Others include the Wo Group (20,000 members and a major base in San Francisco) and the United Bamboo Group, which is based mainly in Taiwan with 10,000 members.

The Code of Ethics of the United Bamboo Members was confiscated by the Los Angeles Country Sheriff's Department in the 1990s:

1. Harmony with the people is the first priority. We have to establish good social and personal connections so as not to create enemies.

2. We have to seek special favours and help from uncommitted gang members by emphasizing our relationships with outside people. Let them publicize us.

3. Gambling is our main financial source. We have to be careful how we handle it.

4. Do not take it upon yourself to start things and make decisions you are not authorized to make. You are to discuss and plan all matters with the group and "Elder Brother."

5. Everyone has their assigned responsibility. Do not create confusion.

6. We do not divulge our plans and affairs to outsiders, for example to our wives, girlfriends, etc. This is for our own safety.

7. We have to be united with all our brothers and obey our Elder Brother's orders.

8. All money earned outside the group must be turned over to the group. You must not keep any of it for yourself. Let the Elder Brother decide.

9. When targeting wealthy prospects, do not act hastily. Furthermore, do not harass or threaten them. Act to prevent suspicion and fear upon their part.

10. If anything unexpected happens, do not abandon your brothers. If arrested, shoulder all responsibility and blame. Do not involve your brothers.

The main criminal activities of Triads include drug trafficking, gambling, money laundering, extortion, prostitution, alien smuggling, and computer chip theft. The core Triad criminal activity is gambling, though the most lucrative is international heroin trafficking. Triad controlled cartels are responsible for more than $200 billion generated from an area in Asia consisting of Thailand, Laos, and Myanmar, known as the Golden Triangle, from which about 50 percent of the world's heroin is supplied.

Trilateral Commission

THIS IS A public offshoot of the Council on Foreign Relations (CFR; see page 36) but with two important distinctions: First, it brought the Japanese ruling elite into the inner circle of global power brokers. Second, it is the brainchild of David Rockefeller. Its website (www.trilateral.org) states its "public" aims:

"The Trilateral Commission was formed in 1973 by private citizens of Europe, Japan and North America to help think through the common challenges and leadership responsibilities of these democratic industrialized areas of the wider world."

It fails to mention that most of these "private citizens" are the richest and most influential individuals on the planet, and that all of the 350 members have been hand-picked by David Rockefeller. Neither does it explain that it was given the stamp of approval at a secret Bilderberg meeting (see page 20) in April 1972 in the tiny Belgian town of Knokke-Heist.

The website also says that, "originally established for three years, our work has been renewed for successive triennia (three-year periods), most recently for a triennium to be completed in 2006." This cleverly gives the impression that its tenure is limited and thus reduces the significance of its extensive and continuing stranglehold on domestic and foreign policy.

Many members of "David Rockefeller's newest international cabal" (*With No Apologies*, by Senator Barry Goldwater) are also Bildeberger and/or CFR members. They have headquarters in New York, Paris, and Tokyo, and they meet once a year in one or other of the regions. Their house publication is called *Trialogue,* and it publishes "Triangle Papers" that are in the public domain.

Rockefeller was heavily influenced by the research of Zbigniew Brzezinski, who was the head of the Russian Studies department at Columbia University. Brzezinski wrote in *Foreign Affairs* (see page 40), and later in his book *Between Two Ages*, that balance-of-power politics needed to be replaced with world-order politics. Brzezinski and many others within the CFR believed that national sovereignty was "no longer a viable concept," and he also supported a "global taxation system."

In the *Wall Street Journal*, David Rockefeller has claimed that the Trilateral Commission is "in reality, a group of concerned citizens interested in fostering greater understanding, and co-operation among international allies." In a letter to the *New York Times* he stressed that "there are about as many Republicans and Democrats, and most regions of the nation are represented." Which is another way of shifting focus away from the core issue—that the Commission members are one-worlders above all else. He continued, "We try to select only the most able and outstanding citizens from the industrial democracies. In that context, it is gratifying and not at all surprising that many former members are now Administration officials."

Even allowing for the merit of Commission members, that alone does not credibly explain the presence of so many of them in every administration since President Carter (17 of his top officials were from the Trilateral Commission). As far back as July, 1973, Brzezinski had highlighted in *Foreign Affairs* the importance "for a Trilateralist to soon become President." Carter's election may have been a miracle, but it was no accident.

Seven months before the Democratic nominating convention, a Gallup Poll showed less than four percent of Democrats supporting him for president. His fortunes changed once David Rockefeller and Brzezinski shoe-horned him into the White House. The irony is that Carter campaigned as a man of the people who was outside the Establishment, when in fact he was Rockefeller's golden boy and the first Trilateral president.

Senator Barry Goldwater explains: "They mobilized the money power of the Wall Street bankers, the intellectual influence of the academic community—which is subservient to the wealth of the great tax-free foundations—and the media controllers represented in the membership of the CFR, and the Trilateral."

In 1980, in an attempt to make the activities of the Trilateral Commission more transparent, Congressman Larry McDonald introduced resolutions in the House of Representatives calling for a congressional investigation, but they came to nothing. His very vocal criticism of secret societies ended abruptly on

September 1, 1983—he was one of the 269 passengers aboard Korean Airlines Flight 007, which strayed off course over a Soviet missile installation in the far Pacific and was shot out of the sky.

It is important to remember in all this that the Trilateral Commission is also a front organization for the Council on Foreign Relations to defuse criticism about its secrecy, but it wasn't the first. In 1925 the CFR established the American Institute of Pacific Relations, which heavily influenced United States policy towards Russia, China, and Japan. It was investigated in 1951 by the McCarren Committee, a Senate Judiciary Subcommittee on Internal Security, but unfortunately this did not result in a wider examination of the CFR. Today it appears that the Commission's role to take the focus away from the CFR, and protect it from the scrutiny of a congressional investigation.

Perhaps the situation is best summed up by a flippant remark of Winston Lord (president of the CFR from 1977 to 1985) and one time assistant secretary of state to the United States State Department : "The Trilateral Commission doesn't run the world, the Council on Foreign Relations does that!"

Epilogue

Now that you have finished this book you are probably thinking, "If everything I have read is true, and they are so powerful, how come they allowed it to be published at all? Why didn't they suppress such highly sensitive information?"

That's easy. They rely on self-censorship. Refusing to believe what we cannot comprehend, or to ignore that which frightens us is human nature.

Still unconvinced?

How many reasons have you already invented to reassure yourself that none of this is true?

Index